# HAUNTED VILLAGE AND VALLEY

ISBN: 978-0-578-06164-1

Rowe Publishing
Washington, D.C.

Printed in the United States of America

Cover photographer: Linda Richters
Cover designer: Jennifer Rogers

To Adele ~
who followed in my footsteps


And, to the Ghosts ~
who beckon us all

## ALSO BY ADI-KENT THOMAS JEFFREY

*The Bermuda Triangle*
*Triangle of Terror*
*They Dared the Devil's Triangle*
*Parallel Universe*
*Ghosts in the Valley*
*More Ghosts in the Valley*
*Across Our Land From Ghost to Ghost*
*Ghosts of the Revolution*
*Witches and Wizards*
*They Dared Niagara*

# HAUNTED VILLAGE AND VALLEY

### A Ghostly Journey Through New Hope and the Delaware Valley

Adi-Kent Thomas Jeffrey
Lynda Elizabeth Jeffrey

# AUTHOR'S NOTE

New Hope is a small historic village nestled along the banks of the Delaware River in southeastern Pennsylvania. It is located midway between Philadelphia and New York City. Its neighboring "sister town," Lambertville, borders the river on the New Jersey side.

The natural beauty of the New Hope area was first seen and appreciated by the Lenni-Lenape Native Americans thousands of years ago. During the years of the Revolutionary War, this region played a pivotal part in our nation's history. In the mid-1800s, the New Hope area was one of the stops along the Underground Railroad for fugitive slaves seeking freedom. During the twentieth century, the village became a gathering place for artists who called themselves the "Pennsylvania Impressionists." Writers, musicians and actors also flocked to the area. A number of luminaries, including James Michener, Dorothy Parker, Pearl Buck, Moss Hart, George S. Kaufman, Oscar Hammerstein and Stephen Sondheim all called the New Hope area their home at one time or another. Grace Kelly made her theatrical debut on the stage of the Bucks County Playhouse. Today, New Hope continues to be a vibrant, diverse, and eclectic town overflowing with an abundance of creative energy.

The borough of New Hope, which consists of one square mile and only four main streets, holds within its borders all of this rich historical, cultural, and artistic legacy. Can there be any doubt that a powerful psychic residue also permeates the atmosphere and environment?

No wonder this little river town has been aptly dubbed, *The Most Haunted Village in America.*"

# CONTENTS

# FOREWORD

My mother, Adi-Kent Thomas Jeffrey, was Bucks County's original ghost chaser! She was a bright, beautiful and fearless woman, filled with joie de vivre and a bold sense of adventure.

My mother spent over forty years researching and writing about supernatural phenomena all over the world, but she always returned to her beloved Bucks County because she believed that no place on earth was more abundant with haunted spirits than the Delaware Valley area. She concluded that the village of New Hope, in particular, was saturated with more ghosts and specters and supernatural manifestations than any other place in the world.

My mother was a brilliant researcher, and a probing reporter. She set out each day with her notebook in hand to explore and to document the eerie happenings in the Delaware Valley area.

The result of her investigations led her to compile the true tales that she had gathered into an anthology of ghost stories. Her two books, *Ghosts in the Valley*, and *More Ghosts in the Valley*, published in the early 1970s, presented her readers with authentic accounts of haunts and spirits that lurked along the dark side of the Delaware. Both of these books are now considered classics. They were recently republished to delight a whole new generation of readers.

Undoubtedly, Adi-Kent Thomas Jeffrey will be best remembered for her book, *The Bermuda Triangle*, which soared to the number one spot on the New York Times Best Seller List and brought her instant notoriety.

During her lifetime, my mother authored over ten books on psychic phenomena. She was a well-known expert in all aspects of the paranormal, but what separated her from so many others in the field was her theory and approach to the supernatural. She was a firm believer in the power of thought. She believed that all ghostly manifestations have their roots in subconscious thought. She also believed that thoughts and energy impressions from the past remain in the mental environment. She concluded that there was always a connection, or an affinity, between the supernatural manifestation and the witness—albeit a subconscious one.

Clearly, my mother was a woman ahead of her time. Decades later, many researchers in the fields of psychology, neuroscience, quantum physics, and metaphysics are making continued discoveries that support her views. We are just beginning to have a deeper understanding of the exquisite mystery and power of our own minds and the many layers of consciousness.

My mother's endless fascination with the supernatural world, along with her conviction that New Hope, Pennsylvania, was "the most haunted square mile in the world," led her to begin another successful venture. In 1982, she founded the company Ghost Tours of New Hope. Swinging her candle-lit lantern, and looking like the New York fashion model that she once was, my mother would lead people from one haunted site to another. Her chilling accounts of genuine spooks and supernatural spirits put New Hope on the map as a desired destination for ghost seekers.

My mother spent a lifetime chasing ghosts. She never paused for even a second… until she went to join them.

But her voice lives on, the voice of a master storyteller and psychic investigator, as she presents her readers for one last time with a collection of true ghost stories. This book represents a fusion of her talents as a researcher, a journalist, and a storyteller. You will observe a blend of writing styles as she recounts ghostly legends, documents historic haunted sites, and investigates recent paranormal encounters. For the first time ever, she also gives readers a peek into her own supernatural experiences.

As I worked to prepare my mother's last manuscript for posthumous publication, you will notice that I've added my own updates or included additional relevant information at the end of some stories. For those readers who are interested in learning more about my mother's beliefs and philosophy pertaining to paranormal experience, I've also added an Appendix which includes excerpts taken from a one-on-one interview with her.

My mother said she wrote her ghost stories to satisfy the natural human desire to "dip into the Great Unknown," as well as to give her readers "a little bit of delicious terror." She believed that ghosts were enticing, intriguing, and entertaining. She said she did not write ghost stories for "analysis."

I'm afraid that I don't entirely agree with her on that last point. In this day and age, I believe a great number of people are eager to explore the supernatural at a deeper level. There are many "seekers" out there who are not afraid to ask questions, ponder new possibilities, and think about things in a different way. For this reason, I decided to include my mother's unusual, and what I would call "enlightened" views and interpretations of supernatural phenomena.

My mother called death the "inevitable adventure." I am sure that her vibrant spirit still floats and glides and dances over the rolling hills of Bucks County, the place she loved most in this earthly world, as she continues her adventures along the never-ending, onward and upward spiral of life.

*Lynda Elizabeth Jeffrey*

The most beautiful thing we can experience
is the mysterious.

\*

*Albert Einstein*

# INTRODUCTION

Ghosts.

The very word conjures up swirling mists in the minds of most people. Do phantasms exist? Many feel they do. And, if so, could they possibly assemble together in one locale in a kind of favorite "haunting ground"? I believe they can, and have, right here in the Delaware Valley area. I have found no place on earth that has a richer, more historic, more meaningful, more colorful past than Bucks County and its environs. I believe ghosts are gathered here because they once lived here—as people. Today they are seen or felt or sensed once again... memories of the past.

I first moved to Bucks County many years ago, and like most visitors and residents, I was naturally attracted to the lull of the river and the beauty of the landscape. One of the first things I hastened to do was to drive up and visit New Hope. Well known as an artists' colony, I found it to be all that I had anticipated. There were shops brimming with copper wares and hand blown glass; artists with their easels set upon the corners painting the town's old buildings and its picturesque bridges; barges going up and down the canal; and the waters of the Delaware glimmering in the sunlight.

Little did I dream that one day I would find much more to see than what appeared on the surface. In the decades that followed, a whole barrage of strange and wonderful stories opened up to me... of people and places and houses all filled with haunting memories. These accounts of mysterious happenings so fascinated me that I eventually compiled them into two volumes of ghost stories— *Ghosts in the Valley* and *More Ghosts in the Valley*. An interlude of fifteen years elapsed during which I was busy exploring supernatural phenomena around the world, writing, lecturing, and finally setting up a new home in Washington, D.C. Then the inevitable happened—the ghosts from the dark side of the Delaware called me back again. There were more stories and legends just waiting to be told.

I invite you to join me for a chilling encounter with a variety of shadowy folks from the netherworld who have found this historic and scenic area so alluring that they decided to stay... forever.

*Adi-Kent Thomas Jeffrey*

# GHOSTLY ECHOES FROM THE PAST

The lawn
Is pressed by unseen feet, and ghosts return
Gently at twilight, gently go at dawn,
The sad intangible who grieve and yearn...

*

*T.S. Eliot*

# LOVE CROSSED THE DELAWARE

*Vintage engraving, Washington's historic crossing of the Delaware on December 25, 1776*

All day it had been clear. Now it was past eleven of the clock and a storm was blowing in, spinning with sleet. Captain Smith plunged one worn boot into the boat and held on to his tricorn hat as he elbowed forward to the prow of the boat.

The Delaware was jammed with ice. Huge chunks hurled along in the river's wind-whipping flow. The Captain peered through the sleet at the boat readying itself next to his. He could just make out the erect form of the Commander-in-Chief. Washington was gesticulating wildly. Smith could catch just a few of the General's words—"surprise"… "the Jersey side"… "await the artillery"… all parts of the big pattern. Tonight, Christmas Eve, the Continental Army was making a desperate man's move: crossing the ice-laden Delaware to march on Trenton.

Smith steadied himself as the boat rocked on impact with a block of ice. He wrapped his cloak tighter around him, bending his head against the needle-sharp sleet. He began to think of the last time he'd bent his head against the snow, only a few weeks before, with *her* hand in his as they plunged through the knee-high drifts and the British bullets shattered all about them into snow-crusted pine trees.

The very thought of her warmed this frozen hour. Emma Read. Beautiful Emma Read, the prettiest, most sought-after girl in Burlington, New Jersey. And she was his. All his. As soon as the war was over and his obligations to his country fulfilled, he would return to Burlington and marry her. Emma Smith, she would be then. He ducked his numb chin deeper into the high collar of his cloak and mused: Emma Smith. Beautiful lass. Beautiful name. Beautiful thought.

A curse cut the wild air and carried over to him now. Shielding his eyes from the wild, icy flakes, he quickly took note of a fellow comrade in need. A soldier had lost the rags wrapped about one foot, whipped off in a lurch of wind cutting across the boat. Smith tore off the bottom of his cloak and with a quick pitch, he tossed it across to the soldier.

He remembered how the snow had cut across their faces a few weeks ago when he and Emma made their escape through Burlington. He had been a prisoner in the British barracks, sitting by the window awaiting shipment to New York for trial as a spy, because he'd been captured out of uniform trying to get through the British lines to Emma's house. He should have known the barrack commander would have the Read house well surrounded. Major Morton was himself a suitor of Emma's hand and was determined to remove all opposition. That day he had done so. Captain Smith was captured and imprisoned at the barracks.

Smith smiled now while the wind froze his cheek bones and the sound of the oars striking ice grated in his ears. Major Morton certainly thought he had held the trump card that night. He'd taken great delight in calling on Emma and telling her of the rebel's capture. This only sharpened the rebel in Emma. Immediately after the major departed, she donned her cloak and made her way through snow drifts as high as a musket's barrel over to the British barracks.

As soon as the Redcoats were occupied with midnight change of guards, she threw a stone at the window where Smith was sitting. At the right split second when there was no guard at his elbow, he opened the window and bolted out into the veil of whirling snow.

Hand in hand, he and Emma plunged through the storm of ice

bullets until they were lost in a maze of pines bordering the Delaware. That night they'd hidden out at a patriot's house on the east side of Burlington. The next day Smith rejoined Washington's forces digging in on the Bucks County side. The Captain had taken Emma in his arms with vows of returning to her as soon as victory was theirs. Little did Captain Smith know that his return to New Jersey would be so soon... and victory over the enemy so imminent.

Here it was a few days later and he was obeying General Washington's orders to do the impossible—cross the frozen Delaware and surprise Trenton!

Finally the deed was done. The boats grated to a stop on the Jersey shore. Within a few hours the entire army of a few thousand men was on the march for Trenton. The Hessian forces, taken by surprise, were overcome within three quarters of an hour.

For Captain Smith there was a surprise, too.

A British major stepped out of a building into his path. Smith raised his sword and swung. The British officer's plumed helmet rolled off his head as he dropped dead on the ground.

It was Major Morton.

Years later, victory for the patriots was complete, and Captain Smith returned to Burlington and made Emma Read his wife. The story of their courtship and romance has been told by the children of Captain and Emma Smith to their children and then down through the generations to the present day.

Does Major Morton's ghost still return to Burlington because of his tragic losses?

Some say he does. For it was here, in what was once a village, that the British officer lost the love of his life—Miss Emma Read. People say there is no mistaking the ghostly apparition of a lone officer, clad in a brass-buttoned scarlet coat, tight-fitting khaki knickers, and worn jack boots who appears occasionally traipsing along the shadowy footpaths in the frozen, empty night. An unhappy soul still haunted by lost love? A restless spirit returning once more to seek revenge against a bold-hearted rebel?

Ah! The story of Captain Smith and Miss Emma Read... fact or legend, who knows for certain? But there is evidence of one thing sure. Someone in the British barracks at Burlington thought all through their waiting days of beautiful Emma Read. Many years ago, when the old barracks were taken down, a passer-by picked up a pane of glass from one of the old barracks' windows. Etched across the corner of the window pane were the words: "Emma Read, Belle of Burlington."

*

*The Burlington Barracks were originally constructed in 1759 to house British troops during the French and Indian wars. The stone barracks were located on East Broad Street. The Catholic Church purchased the building in 1845. Saint Paul's Church stood on the site for many years. According to Burlington historian, George DeCou, "the side walls of the church were the walls of one wing of the barracks." Today the old building is occupied by the Knights of Columbus.*

## A KING'S CURSE

In a distant woods, off the main highway in Buckingham Township, a wooden springhouse stands unnoticed in a frame of hickory and beech trees. Under the limestone rocks, almost forgotten by the townspeople, bubbles one infamous spring, which centuries ago the Indians named "Konkey Hole."

The natural spring came into being, tradition says, over 300 years ago when a Delaware Indian settlement existed in the valley of Lahaska. One day when a brave was skinning a deer, the limestone crust beneath suddenly gave way and they pitched into the water-filled depths. From that moment on, the Indian never ceased to wander the vast subterranean caverns, seeking the place of his ingress, and Holicong established its reputation as one of Bucks County's most haunted territories.

Following on the heels of this tale came the story of the Indian, who, having stabbed a buck with his knife, jumped onto the animal's back to finish the deed. With an amazing leap, the maddened animal plunged into the same mysterious, watery abyss. The noble buck swam through an underground network of caverns, surfacing at Aquetong Lake, nearly three miles away. The Indian, not so fortunate, remained trapped with his other-brother spirit to haunt the bubbling waters of Holicong.

The most troublesome haunter of this area, however, was to be the chief of the tribe, King Hickoqucom. This hot-blooded king was the son of the great Tammany and chosen by him to be his successor. Every land purchased by the English had to be wrested from Hickoqucom.

In 1682, the chief agreed to sell land to William Penn's cousin and agent, Governor William Markham. After making the deal, however, the Indian king felt betrayed by what he considered the unjust and fraudulent practices of the officials who were serving as the proprietaries of Pennsylvania. He was troubled to see white men settling on Indian lands for which they had never received payment.

Two years later, in a fit of regret over the deal, King Hickoqucom sought out an English settler, John Chapman, and angrily declared he was on Indian property. Before leaving England, Chapman had purchased five hundred acres of land "to be laid out in Pennsylvania." After making the arduous trip to America, John, his wife, and their three children, took up residence in the woods of Wrightstown. Setting up their household goods in a cave, they were the first white settlers to penetrate the wilderness north of Newtown. According to King Hickoqucom, however, they had settled on a tract of land to which the Indian title had not been extinguished. In a fit of rage, he confronted the new white settlers. He proclaimed that "the right to the soil of this Province is in the native Indians and not in the Crown or its Grantees. No title is good, but that from the Indians." He then punctuated the announcement of Chapman's land violation with a toss of his ax onto the spot of ground he considered the true boundary!

The last mention of Hickoqucom in the Colonial Records states that he attended a Council held in Philadelphia in 1701. After this last fruitless fight for the rights and titles of Indian lands, legend has it that Hickoqucom returned to his people and took the only course of action left. With a sudden lunge before the very eyes of his subjects, he sank into the bottomless Holicong hole, dooming his spirit to avenge the white inhabitants forever more, as his body had while living. Thus did the great spring become the abode of the "mighty and mischievous spirits of Holicong."

Extraordinary, strange phenomena that have happened at diverse times in this territory seem to prevail unto this day. "What else," wrote a historian of the last century, "engenders the mischief so long afflicting the area... suspicion, discord, slander, law suits. What else causes sinkholes to appear, the caving-in of wells, the hidden streams and the mysterious lights that flickered around them all—

traps to allure the unwary? Wicked and troublesome spirits that once inhabited the surface must be the cause of the inexplicable, supernatural occurrences that haunt the whereabouts of this small hamlet."

*The Indian Chief vowed that his spirit would come back to haunt the Delaware Valley.*

Now, covered from the unwary feet and prying eyes, the cursed waters of the Holicong spring continue to bubble unknown, but the "mighty and mischievous spirits" trapped below the fathomless depths have never ceased to make their presence known.

\*

*The village of Holicong (located roughly between New Hope and Doylestown) was originally called "Hollekonk" in Indian times. It takes its name from the large spring of water (limestone sink-hole) around which the Lenni-Lenape camped. This curiosity, on Holicong Road between Valley Farm and Barley Sheaf Farm, is a funnel-shaped depression, which is about 120 ft. across at the top, and from 30 – 50 ft. down to the water. The spring rises and falls within the funnel. An Indian legend has it that if a tribesman dropped a barley sheaf into Konkey Hole, that same leaf would mysteriously resurface at Ingham Spring near Aquetong, three miles away.*

Today the house is no more. It was demolished decades ago. A modern bank now stands on the site just north of Bristol Pike in Andalusia, Pennsylvania.

During the Revolution, this stretch of land was nearly as active as it is today. Bristol Pike was once called the King's Highway. It was a much-used route by travelers, coaches and post messengers carrying news from colony to colony.

Many sojourners along this path spent the night or stayed for dinner at the Red Lion Inn, the first public house in the area. Located on the King's Highway across from the Poquessing Creek, this tavern was the ideal stopping place for wayfarers enroute to and from Philadelphia and New York. Such historic guests included the Massachusetts delegation to the First Continental Congress in 1774. Samuel Adams made the inn his watering hole, as did the notorious John Adams, who frequented the inn on his travels to and from Pennsylvania.

Looking back in history, we know that these were desperate times for our fledgling nation. By 1777, the cause of the Rebels was in deep trouble. That September, along Brandywine Creek near Chadds Ford, General Washington's attempt to halt the advancing Redcoats had failed. He withdrew to Valley Forge for a rugged winter encampment; the British, under Sir William Howe, took Philadelphia.

It was a crushing blow for staunch supporters of the Rebellion in and around the Philadelphia area.

One of the most ardent patriots for the cause of independence lived just a short distance north of the old Red Lion Inn. He eyed every passing Redcoat with burning hatred. His neighbors, both Tories and Rebels, knew the depths of his resentment. His daughter, too, was well aware of how he felt. She made certain to avoid talking about the recent capture of Philadelphia by the enemy.

From time to time, her father would invite other zealous patriots in the nearby region to come to his house. Hours would fly by as the impassioned men sat in front of a roaring hickory wood fire, discussing the principles of liberty and the importance of supporting the Rebels' cause.

It was on one such occasion as this, that a man in the group reported a disturbing fact: a young girl in the area was having a romance with a British officer. The couple had been seen after dark down in the wooded stretches of the Poquessing Creek not far from the Red Lion.

Rising up from his chair with eyes ablaze, her father was the first one to denounce such an act of betrayal. "A girl of our likes daring to engage in such despicable behavior with a loathsome Redcoat!" He felt the repulsion surge to his tightening scalp as he reached for his gun over the hearth. "Why, such a gentlewoman might as well be consorting with the Devil himself!"

This unforgivable act, he believed, deserved death and eternal damnation.

The moon pulled back behind heavy clouds as the man plunged noiselessly through wet, rotted leaves in the woods behind his house. He would search the banks of the creek, personally, himself, tonight. He edged towards the back of the Red Lion when a sound halted him. A young girl's laughter floated through the night air. It came from the creek below. He edged down slowly towards the muffled sounds. At that precise moment, the brilliance of the full moon caught the crimson and gold braid of a Redcoat uniform.

The man raised his gun, aimed and fired. With a choking sound the officer fell. The girl shrieked. Her figure stood out in perfect silhouette as she leaned over the fallen soldier.

The man raised his gun again. There was no cry now as the slim form in full skirts sank to the ground.

Threading his way down through the wooded ravine, the patriot stalked towards his fallen prey.

He gave the body of the Redcoat a swift kick, grunting to himself with a sense of satisfaction. Then he turned towards the form of the young girl. She was moaning, still half-alive. He pulled her up, the hair falling away from her face. And then, for a few seconds, his heart stopped beating. His face froze in horror. It was his daughter!

With trembling hands, he quickly lifted her up into his arms, dropping his gun by the dead soldier. He carried his precious child back to the house, staggering forward with each heavy footfall in complete disbelief. "You!" he murmured in agony. "How could it have been you! How could I have... my own beloved daughter!"

He reached the front door, shoved it open and started up the stairs towards her room. Halfway up the steps, she gasped one last breath and was gone in an instant.

By the time he placed his daughter on the soft coverlet of her bed, she was dead.

Grief stricken and broken-hearted, the father chose to live out the remainder of his days as a recluse.

The rest of the war for independence was fought and won, but her father was not the rousing hand of cheer he had been. He was a man of suffering. The house became a house of sorrow filled with nothing but remorseful tears and an unrelenting chill.

*Haunted Stairway. Tragic and emotionally-charged events of the past have been known to permeate the atmosphere of an old building with intense psychic energy.*

For centuries to follow, the house on the ancient King's Highway never changed its mood of anguish and despair. It haunted every single occupant. Until a few years ago, one still experienced, as had all the inhabitants of the house since the Revolution, a cold draught of air sweeping by at exactly the halfway point on the stairs—a chilling reminder of a young girl's last dying breath.

Today the house, the staircase, and the sweep of mysterious air are gone. But the story of a young Colonial lass and her ill-fated romance with a Redcoat lives on and on.

*

*The Red Lion Inn opened in 1726. The Inn was operational until it burned to the ground on the morning of December 26, 1991.*

## THE GHOST IN ARMOR

Holicong is a quiet town. There one sees the willows stroke the wind and sweep the by-paths with their feathery fingers. Cool springs, meadow pathways and placid farms greet the passerby.

But Holicong is not to be taken at face value. Not on moonlit nights when every corner of its serene confines is swept free of comforting warmth and the bold blacks of its trees, fences, and tombstones pierce the moon-ice in frightful silhouette.

Then beware! Those are the hours of strangeness for the stoutest heart; the time for peering backwards over the shoulder. It is the period of silence which is not silent at all. It is the hour which belongs to the gentle ghost who is rarely gentle, the Quaker knight in armor who rattles up Old York Road on his white steed or, in his more subdued moments, merely paces the graveyard of the Quaker Meeting House in town where his grave lies deep but unrestraining.

Who is this unique ghost who is at once Quaker and combatant, gentle and rollicking, fascinating and frightful? He is Nathaniel Bye who was born in Southwark, England, in 1677. When he was a young man, he started a career of military bravado, fighting for King William III. His battles took him far and wide. He fought, so the tale goes, for his king in England, Holland and France. Upon his father's death, Nathaniel came to the new world to take over the family homestead in Pennsylvania. He settled down in Bucks County with his wife, Martha, and their children. The armor was put away. Perhaps it was done so as a symbol of "burying" all that was foreign to his new way of life as a quiet Quaker resident of Bucks.

Nathaniel hid from his family and himself his stout, scarred armor. No one ever knew what was in the locked, paneled oak box which he forbade to be opened. All was serene in the Bye household back in the green reaches near Holicong spring. Nathaniel became a refined gentleman-farmer, living off the proceeds from the limestone quarry on his property. He spent his days governing his prosperous household, hunting the hillsides with his friends, the Lenni-Lenape Indians of the area, and setting up a fur trading business. His closest companion was the tribe's chieftain. Together the two warriors hunted the woods. The tribe loved Nathaniel so much he was adopted. The chief called him "brother."

*A knight in shining armor is said to haunt the highways and byways of Holicong village in Bucks County, Pennsylvania.*

So went Nathaniel Bye's peaceful days until a stormy night in the winter of 1748. The wind pushed down the chimney and thrashed the stone walls of his home. A hard-driven sleet bent the tree tops to its iron will. Inside the Bye home in the upstairs room the old knight lay dying.

"Thomas! John!" he called to his sons. "Fetch me the oak chest! Thee both be quick!"

With wondering eyes the two sons and his wife watched as the father slowly lifted the heavy lid. The Byes were not alone. The Indian "brother" stood, hands folded, at the foot of the bed.

There was no sound, it is said, as the old man lifted a piece of the contents to the flickering light of a fat candle. The smooth metal of a piece of steel armor gleamed back at the staring group. It was a suit of armor within the chest. The fighting armor of Nathaniel Bye, late of Southwark, England.

In short gasps and quickened breath the old man gave orders to his sons to dress him in the armor that he might go to his final resting place sheathed in the gear he had fought so well in and guarded so long as a secret from his family.

Strange closing moments for a Quaker church member and his surprised family.

Yet, not really a closing moment at all. Nathaniel Bye was too much a fighter in spirit as well as flesh to give in to the shadows of the other world. He yet roams the hillside in Holicong, it is said. On moon-dusted nights near the midnight hour he has been seen galloping along Old York Road on his white horse. Some folks passing by the graveyard of the old Buckingham Meeting House, have spotted him roaming among the headstones, pacing in his shining armor, his hand always on the hilt of his sword ready to challenge.

His own burial place lies under a few stones carefully placed by a descendant so that his remains should not go unmarked as the early Quakers believed they should be.

But in a grave either marked or unmarked, Nathaniel Bye will never be one to rest in peace.

In the witching hour of a moon-bright night, this sword-brandishing Quaker takes to the road. He thrashes against the willows, sears the paving of the highway with the steed's storming hooves, and stabs the village's midnight silence with his cries and clatter.

When the moon has gone down, the knight in armor fades into the absorbing silence of the old graveyard. All is ready for the wakeful hour, and under the emerging face of the full sun, the little village of Holicong smiles serenely to greet the new day.

*

*The earliest meetings of the Friends' Society were held at the house of Nathaniel Bye until a nearby place of worship was erected. Buckingham Meeting House, in the nearby village of Lahaska, was founded by Nathaniel's two sons, Thomas and John, in 1721.*

*The original Bye homestead was situated on 600 acres of farm land in*

*Holicong, Pennsylvania. The land was granted to Nathaniel's father (Thomas Bye) in 1699 by William Penn. The Byecroft estate (as it was later called) was passed down from one generation to another. Gerard H. Bye spent the last years of his life looking after the farm complex until his death in 1990.*

## THE SEARCHING GHOST OF BONAPARTE

There is nothing left today of the tall, four-storied mansion of Sarah Lukens Keene on Radcliffe Street in Bristol. But the memory of the great house with its marble mantels, its glimmering paned windows, and its frame of surrounding trees still hovers in the thoughts of many of the old residents in town.

Centuries have passed, and yet tales of its hauntings have continued to this very day.

But first let us recall the background of the mansion. In the early years of the 1800s it was one of the most renowned dwellings in Bucks County. Sarah Lukens Keene lived there. Sarah was a beauty. She was young, vibrant and lighthearted—the toast of every gentleman who passed her way. The great portrait painter, Thomas Sully, made her the subject of one of his finest paintings. It hung for years in the dining room of the old mansion.

Sarah had many an affair of the heart, it is said. Two men once fought a duel over her on the lawn beside the house. It has never been known who they were, or who won or lost the exchange of pistol fire. But neither won the hand of Sarah.

After Napoleon's final fall at Waterloo, his brother, Joseph Bonaparte, the ex-king of Naples and Spain, escaped to America. He acquired over 1,700 acres of land in Bordentown, New Jersey. Joseph transformed the property into a splendid country estate complete with winding carriage drives, lavish trees and shrubbery, picturesque English gardens, a man-made lake dotted by landscaped islands, and a vast network of tunnels that ran beneath the property. At his grand estate, which he named "Point Breeze," Bonaparte entertained many great men of the day, including John Quincy Adams, Daniel Webster, and the Marquis de Lafayette.

It is not surprising to learn that Bonaparte, who enjoyed a grand social life, was also a frequent visitor at the Keene mansion. He would glide down the Delaware River on his eight-oared barge and

*Joseph Bonaparte's ghost still haunts the Delaware riverbanks in Bristol, Pennsylvania.*

dock at the Keene landing with great pomp and ceremony. Many an evening he wined and dined at the glimmering crystal and silver settings in the oval room. Many an hour he told tales by the snapping fire in the great salon. Often he played at chess or listened to merry tunes tinkling from the grand piano in the majestic parlor.

It is reputed that he looked longingly into the soulful eyes of the lovely Sarah. But, alas, she was never to be more than a friend to Joseph Bonaparte.

Whom did Sarah Lukens Keene marry? No one. She gave her heart, it is said, to a man from the hustling city of Philadelphia. A bourgeois man who made beer. Sarah's father put a flat refusal to the courting of Sarah by the beer-maker. Such an unworthy suitor was not to be considered. The man left Bristol and the gleaming halls of Keene mansion. And Sarah's eyes never sparkled again.

Eventually she was alone in the echoing house. There were no more duelists, no more kings at her hearthside, no more balls and dinners of state. Only the shade trees trembling in cold-fingered winds outside the windows and the still, ivory keys of the piano.

Sarah's will said a lot. A lot about loneliness. She left her Bristol mansion to the Episcopal Church. It was to be used as a charitable home for "aged, unmarried gentlewomen who are alone, friendless or helpless."

Today only the river winds brush the grass that long-ago surrounded her glorious estate. The lapping of the gentle waves tells the story of Bristol's nineteenth century beauty along the shore where once her satin-slippered feet stepped on and off Bonaparte's barge. The shade trees still hover over Radcliffe Street and recall that once the sound of dueling pistols shattered the night's silence on that near-by lawn.

But memories of all these past happenings still haunt the thoughts of many in Bristol who recall the Keene mansion. People who can summon up the strange sounds and the eerie moods of the house which eventually led to the name it has carried for decades: The Haunted House of Bristol.

One of these people is Mattie. When I met Mattie she was living on Race Street in Bristol. She was born there in the early 1900s and lived for many decades in a house just behind the place where the Baptist Church now stands. Today Mattie's gray hair frames a strong, black face which smiles graciously at you when she talks. Her posture is straight; her manner is dignified, yet warm. Pensively, she reflects back on the years she spent in the Keene mansion. Not one of the caretakers would stay there without Mattie.

"It is understandable," she says with a gentle nod of her head. "There was no place more—more shivering and eerie at night than that house."

What did she experience there? Footsteps treading distinctly across the floors. Doors opening in the dead of night and clicking shut. Dishes rattling in the kitchen. All sounds and echoes made one *sure* someone was walking in the house at night. But when a light was snapped on—no one would be there. One of the caretakers slept with the lights on—few slept at all. It was more common that two or more would be awake in the night and sit up together. One evening, the tympanic rhythm of firm steps was heard outside the house on the river side stalking back and forth all night long.

Was this one of the duelists? Did he seek the man who killed him in the darkness of the night so long ago? Was it Bonaparte pacing the walk waiting for the lovely mistress of the Keene mansion? Does Sarah tread the rooms of her old home, seeking her lost lover?

No one knows the cause of the hauntings, or who the restless spirits were that stirred through the mansion. Perhaps it could be any of the people who spent happy or sad hours in the magnificent home. In the late years of the last century, the Keene house was so feared for its hauntings, no one would walk past it. People would cross the street, then back again. Mattie recalls this well.

The newspapers of the day recorded that weird green lights were seen flickering from room to room on the darkest nights. It was said to be the ghost of Joseph Bonaparte, moving from room to room, lantern in hand, revisiting scenes from his past and the lavish hospitality of the hostess he admired so much.

Look carefully when you walk along the river's edge behind the Grundy Library. Are those green lights shimmering from the water reflections or phosphorous glows? Or are they from the lantern of Bonaparte's ghost as he glides away on his elaborate river boat still feeling the afterglow of a happy evening spent in the company of Miss Sarah Lukens Keene?

\*

*The Sarah Lukens Keene Home for Aged Gentlewomen was put into operation in 1874, following the directives Miss Keene outlined in her will. The home was eventually torn down in the 1960s to make way for the Margaret R. Grundy Library.*

*The only vestiges of the original "Point Breeze" estate are the tunnel to the river and the house Bonaparte had built for his trusted secretary, Louis Maillard. Since Bonaparte's death, the property has changed hands several times. The last acquisition was made by the Divine Word Missionaries in 1941.*

# FLEA MARKET FIND

Searching for a good bargain or a special treasure? Throughout the years, the Bucks County flea markets have attracted thousands of folks who enjoy hunting for second-hand goods, vintage items, antiques, and all kinds of collectables and memorabilia.

On many a weekend, my daughter and I would visit the Golden Nugget Antique Market in Lambertville, New Jersey, ambling around from booth to booth, hunting and gathering, wheeling and dealing. Occasionally, on a Tuesday morning, we would rouse ourselves out of bed at the crack of dawn in order to join the crowds at Rice's Market. This famous county market, located just outside of New Hope, has been in operation for over 100 years and true to its promise, this is a place where "you can buy everything under the sun."

Years ago, there was another smaller flea market which was located in Lahaska, Pennsylvania, directly across from the shops at Peddler's Village. Very close to this site, there was a popular restaurant called the Soup Tureen. My daughter and I would often stop there to grab a bite to eat after a rewarding day of shopping.

One afternoon, after the two of us had spent many hours at the nearby flea market, we decided to treat ourselves to a bit of refreshment at this delightful, colonial-styled restaurant. It was late in the day and the place was practically empty. As Lynda and I sat at the table chit-chatting back and forth, rummaging through our bags of purchases, we happened to strike up a conversation with our waitress, Louise. Before we knew it, she put down her tray, tossed off her ruffled dust cap, and pulled up a chair to our table. Louise then proceeded to regale us with the most amazing flea market story I've ever heard in my whole life.

One day, a customer she was serving, a self-proclaimed flea market addict, told her of an incredible purchase that her friend had made some years ago at the Lahaska Market. It was an antique brooch. Perusing the market together, the two women had spotted the pin on one of their first rounds. It was an unusual piece of jewelry—a gem-encrusted, oval brooch that could also be worn as a pendant. Apparently, the dealer was unable to give them any information about the piece. He couldn't even assure them that the stones were real and not antique paste (glass gems). Accustomed to shopping in flea markets, the women were familiar with a wide diversity in pricing, but the price quoted for this particular piece seemed unusually high, especially considering the fact that the pin came with no guarantee.

After a few minutes of haggling back and forth, the woman most interested in the pin decided it was not a piece worth her investment. Bidding the dealer a courteous farewell, the two women turned on their heels and continued their bargain-hunting tour through the maze of tables piled high with all kinds of interesting treasures and miscellaneous junk.

A week later the two ladies returned to the Lahaska Flea Market. As her side-kick explained, "If a piece of jewelry keeps calling out your name, you gotta go back and get it, girlfriend."

Luckily, the pin was still there. She ended up paying the dealer a price which she felt was still too high, but because this brooch had become the sole object of her heart's desire, she gladly paid the sum.

When she arrived home that afternoon, she showed the pin to her husband. She even fessed up to him how much she had paid for this frivolous piece of adornment (what a brave woman). Needless to say, he was stunned by the fact that his wife had purchased a piece of jewelry at a rag-tag flea market from an unknown dealer that came with absolutely no guarantee. He shook his head from side to side in utter disbelief. "I'd like to know what this piece of junk is really worth. Certainly not what you just paid for it!"

It didn't matter to her. As the saying goes, "True value is in the eye of the beholder." She had fallen in love with the pin. As far as she was concerned, it was a one-of-a-kind piece. With a good cleaning from a professional jeweler, the woman felt confident it would be a handsome addition to her collection of antique jewelry.

She took her newly acquired trinket to Bailey Banks and Biddle, a famous high-end jeweler that at the time was located on Chestnut Street in Philadelphia. She requested that the pin be cleaned and polished and, just to satisfy her own curiosity, she also asked for an appraisal of its worth.

A few weeks later, she returned to the store to pick up her flea market treasure. Taking her claim check, the sales assistant disappeared for a few minutes and then promptly came back with the store manager.

The manager placed the pin on a black velvet display tray for her close inspection. The woman stopped to catch her breath. What she saw before her now was a gorgeous, dazzling piece of jewelry! Never in her wildest dreams did she ever imagine that the old, worn-out brooch which had looked so dull and cloudy could possibly be restored to such splendor.

"Madame, would you be kind enough to tell me where you purchased this exquisite piece?" he asked. She told him the truth. In spite of his formal, self-contained demeanor, it was clear that the gentleman was shocked. It was the same reaction her husband had displayed when she first showed him the pin. But, unlike her husband, the manager of Bailey Banks and Biddle obviously knew the worth of the brooch. He couldn't believe his ears... "I beg your pardon, Madame. What did you say?" She reasserted the fact that she had purchased the pin at a local flea market.

Handing her a jeweler's magnifying glass, he then turned the piece over and asked her to look carefully at the back of the pin. Squinting through the eye loupe, the woman expected to see a hallmark, but instead she saw only two words: *pour Josephine.*

*The Empress of France; engraving from 1852*

Just as the jewelers suspected, the pin bore a mark of great historical significance. A token of affection for Josephine, from Napoleon. The brooch-pendant eventually received an official certificate of authenticity verifying its identity as an article intended for, or given to, Josephine Bonaparte, the Empress of France.

How did this priceless piece of jewelry find its way to the United States of America, and more specifically, to the Bucks County area? My best guess is that when Joseph Bonaparte escaped from Europe in 1817 and settled down in Burlington, New Jersey, he must have brought with him a casement of family jewels. When Joseph died in 1844, his grandson was put in charge of dealing with the ex-king's magnificent estate. He quickly disposed of the entire estate—all the contents, furnishings, and the art collection which at the time was the finest in America.

Who would ever imagine that one of Josephine Bonaparte's pendants, which must have been sold at auction sometime during the mid-1800s, would eventually end up on a flea market table in Lahaska, Pennsylvania, more than a century later? As I've always said, truth is stranger than fiction.

So, my dear readers, if you're searching for a treasure, I say come to Bucks County. Who knows? You, too, may find a priceless object that still holds haunting echoes from the past.

\*

*The Lahaska Flea Market is no longer in operation, however, interested shoppers can head to one of the largest and finest flea markets in the area, the Golden Nugget. Located in Lambertville, New Jersey, this indoor/outdoor flea market is a "gold mine" of antiques, collectibles, vintage goods, art works and countless treasures.*

# HAUNTED VILLAGE:
# THE LINGERING GHOSTS OF NEW HOPE

And when your children's children think themselves alone
in the silence of the pathless woods,
they will not be alone.
At night, when the streets of your village are silent,
and you think them deserted,
they will throng with the returning hosts that once filled them...
You will never be alone.

\*

*Chief Seattle*

# AFTER THE DUEL

*Aaron Burr served as third Vice President of the United States from 1801-1804*

Aaron Burr, once a young, nineteen year old officer who fought heroically in Washington's Continental Army, went on to lead quite a complex and checkered political life during the years of our country's early republic. But he is most remembered for being caught in one of biggest scandals of American colonial history. In 1804, when Burr was serving as Vice President of the United States, he challenged Alexander Hamilton to a duel in order to settle the question of his honor. On the morning of July 11, the two rivals stood on the heights of Weehawken, New Jersey, and Burr fired the shot which mortally wounded Hamilton.

After the duel, a very unique situation existed. The Vice President of the United States was indicted for murder in New York and New Jersey and was placed on the list of sought after criminals. Burr had to flee New York for his life. He hid in a hay wagon, crossed through New Jersey, came across the Delaware by ferry, and legend says that he stayed and hid out in New Hope for several days.

Some people say that he never left.

Of all the figures that haunt the New Hope area, the ghost of Burr seems to be the one that wanders through the village the most. The slender man dressed in a black silk jacket with glossy dark hair drawn back in a ribboned queue, and blazing eyes staring forth through his wire-rimmed glasses, has been seen wandering the halls of the Logan Inn, descending the steps at a historic house on

Bridge Street and casting a flickering dark shadow as he passes through the streets and alleyways late at night.

But, unquestionably, Burr's favorite hang-out is the old Coryell House located on South Main Street.

*Burr's ghost still haunts the historic Coryell House in New Hope.*

It was in the early 1950s that I first talked with Mrs. Neal who lived in this lovely, old home. At one time this grand home had belonged to John Coryell, the gentleman who owned and operated the Pennsylvania side of the ferry service in this area during the mid to late 1700s. His original eighteenth century home was designed with walled-in gardens, a lovely entrance way, double parlors, a sitting room, and a beautiful staircase with a tiger maple railing.

When I met Mrs. Neal, the house had certainly fallen to the ravages of time, but nevertheless, she took great delight in leading me up the staircase and showing me the secret recessed area off of the second floor stair landing where legend has it that Burr hid out after the duel while waiting for the public furor to die down.

Does Burr's ire over the injustice dealt him at that time by his political enemies still remain in the very air of the Coryell House? Some inhabitants of the house believe so. One young man, Craig Thomas, tells of the night he felt himself dragged furiously across the room as he slept on a floor mat. The force didn't let him go until it had him slammed against the living room door.

Claudia Lane, too, tells her story. One night when she realized she was all alone in the building, she went downstairs, put on the hall light and locked the main door to the house. Then she returned to her apartment upstairs, locking herself in. Late that night, she awakened to hear the hall light switch downstairs click off. Then in the darkness, she heard footsteps ascending the stairs.

Terrified, Claudia called the bartender next door. He told her to crawl out of her bedroom window onto the roof and to drop the front door key down to him. Claudia followed his instructions. Right away, he called for help. Along with the police, the bartender entered the building. They searched every corner of the hallway, including the old Burr hideaway. There was no one.

Aaron Burr also made a dramatic appearance during one of my ghost tours. The particular time was October, near Halloween. One of my most experienced tour guides was leading a group of tourists to visit the Coryell House. As she was talking and telling the story of Burr, she turned and looked at one of the visitors on the tour. She was a woman who was standing close to her side. Suddenly, the woman's face transformed completely into that of a man. Her voice as she spoke became low and guttural. My tour guide noticed it was a very white face with a high forehead and coal black eyes that seemed to burn in this pale face. She was so terrified that she abandoned the group and came rushing back to the Logan Inn where I was waiting. I have no doubt that the ghostly figure who appeared at that moment was none other than Aaron Burr. She gave me a perfect description of his face.

To this day, Burr continues to walk soundlessly and hollowly through the village streets, haunted himself by his own act of violence. Perhaps on one of your visits to New Hope, you, too, might be overcome with a strange sensation that someone is staring at you from behind. This phenomena is called Burr's "Sightless Stare." Turn quickly and look over your shoulder. You might just catch a fleeting glimpse of our nations third Vice President still tormented by his murderous deed after all these by-gone centuries.

*

*The Coryell House, located at 105 South Main Street, was sold to new owners in the late 1970s. They converted the property into a restaurant, bar and nightclub called "Havana." In 2002, they bought the business next door and remodeled the entire building inside and out. Havanas is known as a New Hope "hot spot" for music and live entertainment. In spite of all these changes, Aaron Burr retains his title as "resident ghost" of the property.*

## THE BUCKET OF BLOOD

One of New Hope's most historic structures, dating back to the eighteenth century, is an old stone, stucco-covered building located on upper Mechanic Street. The present day owner of this site, Paul Licitra, is also the owner and proprietor of a well-known restaurant, the Tow Path House, located a level below the street front building. For decades, this restaurant has been known to offer al fresco dining on a picturesque terrace. And throughout all seasons of the year, diners have enjoyed the warmth and rustic coziness of tables clustered around a centrally located open fireplace. The restaurant is filled with a distinctive ambience and energy. But, along with the chatter, and laughter, and melodic sounds drifting from the piano bar, there is also a heavy cloud of mystery that hovers over the Tow Path House. And, as I discovered for myself, the cluster of buildings that adjoin this restaurant are also teeming with ghosts.

At the Tow Path House, in the cellar storage room, both Paul and one of his employees, Angel Fario, have felt a strong presence. Both complained that they felt someone down there was watching them. Angel said she had such an uncomfortable feeling that she would keep looking over her shoulder just to check and make sure that nothing "weird" was going to happen.

In the house next door to the restaurant, a resident supports that same feeling. Paul Casey revealed to me that he has awakened in his bedroom on several occasions, paralyzed—as though numbed by the presence of a terrific energy force. This force manifests itself as a white, glowing mass. He felt that it came from somewhere close by and invaded his room. "I feel strongly that it did not originate here," he said. He told me that he thought it must have come from the "Bucket of Blood" (the name for an adjoining stucco building).

The challenge here was too tempting to postpone. On the spot, I summoned the owner, his close friends, and one stout candle and, as a group, we entered the dark, and for-the-moment, unoccupied premises.

We climbed the stairs. Please picture if you will the flame of a lonely candle flickering, making walking shadows up each step as we maneuvered our way through the dark. Cool draughts of air swept through a few of the aged window panes. Then we reached the uppermost regions—the attic rooms.

It was like entering a wild, crazy, debauched celebration! It seemed the walls themselves were vibrating with energy. The atmosphere had grown from an icy calm downstairs to a hot, head-pounding turbulence upstairs. Both Paul Casey and I felt "shaky," "blinded," "overwhelmed," or "woozy." The blood seemed to race through our heads leaving us dizzy. I said, "I keep getting a message from this room of intense, disorderly activity. A raging, boisterous atmosphere." The very air seemed pulsating with fever, frenzy and violence.

Paul and I talked about the energy that permeated that room as we made our way downstairs and outside. It took quite awhile before we felt our heads start to clear. Paul said he'd felt a pressure that stopped his ears while in that room, as though he had ascended to some great altitude.

But there is an even more ghostly area than the attic room. A secret tunnel lurks under the Bucket of Blood where illicit activity was commonplace. It was said that contraband goods would be moved on and off the barges through this passageway. Under the cover of darkness, the smugglers would unload the unmarked crates filled with such coveted items as liquor, wine, 'baccy (tobacco), tea, laces and silks. Smuggling was a dangerous, but highly profitable, business. The smugglers were known to be rough and ruthless men. They used the threat of violence, and even murder, to ensure silence from the local community. One can imagine many of the brutal outbursts that would be likely to erupt as the smugglers carried on their shady deals. Who knows what murderous doings took place in that dark underground passageway or how many dead bodies were dragged through that gloomy tunnel to be disposed of quickly into the murky waters of the canal?

Since New Hope was one of the stops on the Underground Railroad during the nineteenth century, this secret tunnel was undoubtedly used by runaway slaves who were headed north to Canada in their brave and treacherous search for freedom. Who knows how many fugitive slaves—men, women, and children— suffering from fatigue, hunger, sickness or injury, passed through the confines of this dark tunnel trembling with fear at the thought of being caught by a cruel slave hunter?

No wonder this burrowed passageway still reeks with panic, dread, terror and horror.

*A tunnel (now boarded up) runs underneath the historic building on Mechanic Street known as "The Bucket of Blood."*

Was I surprised by these discoveries? Well, not really...

About ten years ago, I held a séance with a medium named Grace Walker. We sat together in a small upper room located in one of the old buildings close by on the other side of Mechanic Street. (The building used to house the old Cheshire Cat Shop.) Mrs. Walker described for us the sensations that she was picking up. We listened quietly as she declared, "There was a raucous inn or tavern nearby. Very close. A little north of here. It was a wild place. A lot of wining and wenching and loud shouting and singing." She went on to say, "I see two men fighting together on a dirt floor, one of them swinging an axe! A young girl—a serving girl of some sort who worked at the tavern—is fighting for her life. I believe she was finally murdered in the basement and her body was buried there."

Well, I set out the next day to try to corroborate any of these statements that I could. But I had no success. Not for over ten years. Then finally, as I have recounted to you in this story, I got my break-through. My conversations with Paul and others who have lived and worked on these premises led me to keep on investigating. And I'm go glad I did! There is no doubt in my mind that this cluster of buildings still harbors the wild, reckless, unbridled energy of the rugged and rowdy canal boatmen who, centuries ago, would stagger by to take their respite in the tavern and their "comfort" at the brothel above. A trip up to that attic gave me an experience I shall never forget... a swirl of passionate, mad, heady and tempestuous vibrations.

It is hard to believe that this quaint and charming site was once a place filled with such debauchery, drunkenness and the bloodthirsty crimes of smugglers and crooks. No doubt, it was called "The Bucket of Blood" because of the innumerable murders that took place here.

And the tunnel? Who knows what troubled and restless spirits still wander through that dark and musty channel, the unstilled victims of some misfortune. Perhaps, one of them is a young, frightened serving girl still fighting to visit this earthly world again or a trembling, runaway slave still searching for their never found freedom.

*

*The former Tow Path restaurant has been renamed "Tuscany at the Towpath House." This historic eating establishment, located at 18 West Mechanic Street, is currently owned and operated by my mother's dear friend, Paul Licitra.*

## THE TERRIBLE SECRET

In the late evening when the shadows of dusk have already veiled the rows of houses along Ferry Street in New Hope, you may be able to catch an arresting sight: a woman in a blowing nightdress running up the road towards you, her long hair flying away from her face. But don't be surprised, if just as she reaches you, she vanishes into the night nothingness. She always has.

Probably because she doesn't belong out in the street. She belongs to her favorite haunt—the row of stone townhouses edging up the hill hugged tightly together. It is from one of their windows she is usually spied, leaning out, waving her white arms frantically, over and over, in the moonlight.

She is a ghost from New Hope's past. Not quite so far in the past as some of the village's other phantoms, for this young lady was not born when this crossroads was of the most strategic military importance. Nor did the row of stone houses yet stand when this village was a stronghold for Washington's army. It was at this very site, that the Continentals in '76 quickly constructed a temporary fortification when they feared an attack by the British from across the Delaware. Of course, as it turned out, General Washington beat them to the punch and crossed first in his stunning attack on Trenton.

This revolutionary rampart stood at a crucial point overlooking the river. The boat landing and the Ferry Inn below formed the nucleus of a settlement only to the end of the war. By the end of the 1700s, the village shifted from a fort to an industrial center. The man largely responsible for this change was Benjamin Parry.

The son of a Welsh Quaker pioneer and successful miller, young Benjamin moved to this Delaware settlement and built a stone house close to the ferry landing in 1784. It was more than a house, it was a mansion. Across from his home where a creek flowed into the Delaware, Parry's newly purchased grist mill ground its flour so successfully the young industrialist soon added more mills to his thriving business on both sides of the river. He expanded his "empire" to include a saw mill and flax seed and linseed oil mills. Giant wheels churned the waters of local creeks for long hours each day. Their steady splashing during the close of the war years became a symbol of the life blood of this tiny village.

*Residents in the houses along Regent's Row on upper Ferry Street have been disturbed by the sounds of someone knocking loudly on a door, the shrieks and cries of a young baby, and the echoes of a mysterious thud.*

When the grist mill burned down on a windy night in May of 1790, the whole area was in shock. But the indomitable Benjamin Parry quickly rebuilt it with bigger and better hopes than ever

41

before. He dubbed it New Hope Mill. And so, in gratitude for his perseverance, the townspeople changed the village name from Coryell's Ferry to New Hope. And the name stuck.

To accommodate the foreman of his various enterprises, Parry built a string of attached stone houses along Aquetong Creek, probably in the early 1800s. It is to this era that the pale-gowned lady of Ferry Street belongs. From the bits and pieces of hearsay told to me by old time residents I have reconstructed the following story.

One of the Parry foremen who lived in that row of houses was a tough-sinewed, hard-working bull of a man with a beautiful daughter. A widower, the man had lived there with his only child ever since Parry had taken over the local mill and set it to such high prosperity that he was known for miles around. This home was one of the first to be furnished, a fine row house built of colorful, rudimentary stones that came straight from the Pennsylvania fields. The foreman was proud of it, and his daughter, and his own achievement, rising to this point of success in just a few short years.

He deserved the success he often told himself. It helped make up for the long struggling years that had gone before. Years of starvation and uncertainty when there wasn't a cow around or a kernel of corn or a splinter of timber wood that wasn't seized for the Continental Army. His wife never did recover from those flesh-eating years. She died giving birth to a frail little girl a decade after the war. The man swore then and there that he'd never let that tiny form, no bigger than the reach of his forearm, go through what they had. He promised himself she would never have the wants they'd experienced. They were self-sworn commitments that became as much a part of his soul as had his wedlock vows. Though not much of a religious man, he was a man of strong will. His daughter's future security was in his hands and he was determined that nothing would ever interfere with his fondest hopes. He was determined to control her fate with his unrelenting will.

As the girl grew into womanhood, she displayed a fragile beauty admired by all. The father's hopes soared even higher. Maybe even the fine young son of Mr. Parry would cast a glance in the direction of his angel child. The girl was as opposite to her father in temperament as she was in looks. He was stocky and ruddy of complexion; she was ivory-skinned and raven-locked, and where he would pound the floor boards with heavy-booted feet, she would skim around the rooms in creamy-leathered slippers as delicately as a newborn fawn. Where he would seem to shake the ceiling beams shouting in a fit of rage, she could be heard responding with soothing words that everyone declared flowed from her heart like a river of kindness.

But the father's deeply entrenched hopes for his daughter were of no more influence in the course of events to follow than the birds' songs that twittered inconsequentially around the rock-ribbed walls of his house. In fact, the foreman's plans were to be dashed, with fatal results, as brutal as the crushing of a soft newborn animal deliberately destroyed in an iron trap stumbled upon in dark woods.

It all began on a sun-flecked, spring day when the miller's daughter carried her father's lunch basket to him down at the mill. She came lilting through the open doorway, brushing strands of dark hair away from her eyes. A tawny-haired youth looked up and fastened his vivid eyes on her. He was a new hand that had just moved into the county and gone to work in the saw mill.

He was as brash as the March wind that knocked against the tree branches and stirred up the creek waters and equally as attention-getting. The young girl couldn't look away from his wild blue eyes and muscle-carved body as he slowly returned to work. She watched him bending over lengths of oak and feeding them into the saw blade as rhythmically and powerfully as the mill waters plunged from side to side down the sluiceway. In the next moment, her father stamped out from the miller's office where he'd been assisting in the accounts reckoning. With a push on the girl's shoulder to spin her around and out of the mill, he grabbed the lunch basket and sent her speedily on her way.

The look he'd seen on his daughter's face displeased him. With more reasons than he, at that moment, could have reckoned.

As if guided by some unseen force, the two young people came together again, at dusk down by the creek, hidden from view by a profusion of wild blackberry bushes and feathery leafed laurel. The boy was leaving work; she was gathering berries for the evening repast. It was only the first of several clandestine meetings. The girl was too much in love and too fearful of her father to meet freely as most young couples were entitled.

It wasn't long before the young man became quite vexed.

"It's not to my liking, lass, to be meeting you like a whimpering god, hiding in the woods."

"It's the only way," the girl said softly.

"But it's not my way. We should be having the merriest times of our lives, I say! Look, there's a spring dance coming up in Trent's Town across the river. I want to take you and show you the wildest, happiest dancing any man ever put his shoes to."

"My father would never... "

"The deuce with your father. You're a grown woman. I say it's up to you where you go and whom you chose to go with!"

The girl shook her head. "Not in these parts...."

"The Devil take 'these parts,' I'm going to be coming a-calling Saturday night! You be ready now lass!"

Before the girl could protest, he'd sealed her lips with a kiss and bounded off into the woods.

Touching and re-touching his kiss as she made her way to the embankment, the girl gathered fresh courage. Yes, yes, he was right. She should be free to be happy and in love, as she so deeply was.

But bringing up the subject to her father was a different matter. Every time she started to speak he would break into a stormy tirade about the price of cream or the poor workmanship of the shoemaker who repaired his boots. He never seemed to be in a receptive frame of mind. Finally, the girl decided to let her lover come calling as though it were the accepted thing to do. Surely her father would realize the naturalness of two young people to be courting.

That Saturday evening after the dinner chores had been done, the young girl put on her spun linen dress and plaited ribbons in her hair, all the while her heart beating violently against the tiny bone buttons of her bodice. Then the knocks came. Loud knocks on the front door below. Like the young man himself, the pounding was brash and sure and she loved him for his confidence. She stood still a moment, trying desperately to reach out and pull from the presence some strands of his character's bold fabric and weave them into her own.

She ran quickly and looked out of her bedroom window. Her heart beats skipped. He was on the steps below. He was as beautiful as a god. His hair was freshly combed and his fine cut features were shining from hard soap scrubbing. His linsey-woolsey shirt looked like a little boy's Sunday best. She rushed out of her room and down the stairs, tingling with excitement.

At the foot of the stairway her father stood, staring up at her, his hands on his hips.

"Where, pray, daughter, do you think you are going?"

He was uniquely calm but she could see the fire burning behind his eyes.

"I'm going to open the door. I have a young man a-calling."

"You! You've got nothing but gall and nerve and cheek!"

The knocking on the door continued. She felt her face flushing with fear and uncertainty.

"Father, how can you be so certain—sure about—well, you don't even know who he is."

"Do you think I am stupid? As stupid as you, planning as you must have been to team up with a wastrel—a man who will offer you a dance one day and a sod house with bawling brats the next! You'll not take a step out of this house with anyone until I say so!"

The knocking became louder and more persistent. The girl covered her ears as the tears poured down her face. Her father never budged from his stance so she flung back up the stairs, her feet flying without stopping until she reached her room.

She heard the window shutters creaking apart in the parlor downstairs. She knew her father was staring with hatred in his eyes on her forsaken young man.

She pulled herself to the bedroom window again and opened it. The boy looked up at her with disgust on his face. Then he turned on his heels and stalked away.

She never saw him again.

Very few people in the village ever caught sight of the young girl again. She scarcely ever left the house except to gather berries occasionally. Her father did not permit her to come to the mill anymore.

Then one clear night in December the other foremen families knew something was amiss in the widower's house. A baby was heard crying suddenly in the dark hours, followed by a girl's screams. Although several men went to their front doors and their wives peered from behind partially closed shutters, no one dared interfere with the tough, strapping foreman who was not a man to tolerate intrusion into his business and they all knew it.

Suddenly the shutters of an upstairs bedroom in the widower's house flew apart and heavy arms with a small, wailing form caught in them thrust wildly outwards—and just as suddenly, the cries of an infant ceased. There was only a sickening thump on the brick wall below. Then the girl pushed to the window and struggled, her hands clutching to pull herself out. But at that moment the man's arms dragged her back inwards. Her screams faded as the shutters closed again. And there was only silence from the black-engulfed house. Except for the grating of a shovel against brick for a few minutes in the blackest hour of the night.

No one ever saw the foreman and his daughter again. Before dawn a few days later the two were gone. No one knew where. Perhaps to the west where so many unhappy people were moving in those days. The father and his daughter simply faded from sight.

Yet, actually, not altogether.

This tragedy, believed to have taken place almost two centuries ago, accounts for one of the eeriest ghosts of Ferry Street, say some of the residents there. Along the row of stone houses (now called Regent's Row), different occupants over the years have complained of a common occurrence: in the middle of the night they will hear loud knocking on a front door. When they get up to check, there is never anyone there.

One owner told me of her concern when this first happened to her shortly after moving in. "It's terribly unnerving, you know, that loud pounding in the dead of night. At first, I thought I must be hallucinating. It was a comfort when my next door neighbor confided in me that she had experienced the same thing."

Several years ago, I talked to a couple who lived in Regent's Row. They told me of awakening in the middle of the night on one occasion to the sound of a dull thump on the street outside. When they got up and peered out, there wasn't a sign of anything. "Yet," the husband said, "it sounded as though something had been dropped from a great height and had hit the brick paving with a thud." There was a pause and then his wife added with a shudder, "You know, for some reason, it made my stomach turn over. It was chilling."

Then there is the owner of the first house in the row. Dudley Kelley told me that he was constantly hearing footsteps all over his house. Some soft and delicate, like a young girl's, others loud and pounding as though a man was walking heavily on the floor boards. Sometimes he heard them upstairs, walking overhead. Sometimes he heard them downstairs. A frequent guest of his, Bob Miles, told me with a shrug of acceptance, "Oh, there are footsteps around this place all the time. Every time I come here, I hear them. Usually in the middle of the night. I tell you, you kinda get used to it after a while."

As I looked around the shadowy parlor, I recalled being in this same house ten years ago when I was interviewing the owner at the time. She was Nancy Eaton. Nancy and her husband were an unusually busy couple. Along with a crew of workmen, they had just finished restoration work on the row of mill homes, converting the place into a motel. Although open for only a brief time, the Eatons were doing well and had already had such notable guests as Dorothy Lamour and her husband. Besides running Regent's Row, the couple had a baby to care for. It was a case of the right hand working at one thing while the left tended to further chores.

One evening at dusk, Nancy had just finished registering a couple when she heard loud wails coming from upstairs. Her husband came in through the front door at just that moment. "Say, hon, will you go see what's wrong with the baby?" Nancy blurted out. "I've heard nothing but crying for over five minutes and it's driving me crazy, I can't take it one second more!"

Her husband bounded up the stairs. In seconds he was back. His face was white.

"What's the matter? Is the baby okay?"

"Gregory wasn't crying, Nancy!" he blurted. "In fact, the second I approached the bedroom door, the howling stopped abruptly. But it wasn't Gregory! I swear to you, he was sound asleep." Nancy looked at me and shrugged. "You can believe it or not. That's what happened. And I'll tell you, I don't go much for all this crock about spooks and spirits and such. To me, anyone who says he's seen a ghost is full of beans. But, I swear, that's a true story about the baby crying upstairs. I can't explain it to anyone—least of all myself. But, the bottom line is—there was a loud sound of a baby wailing from that front bedroom and it wasn't my kid!"

I told Nancy I believed her.

As I stepped out the back door and stood facing the wooden ravine behind the stone houses, Nancy, her gaze catching up with mine, caught her breath. "You know when the crew was first clearing the backyard here, one of the workmen tearing down the old outhouse, unearthed a grisly thing. He found buried in years of accumulated debris, a tiny baby's skull."

I stared at her.

"That tells us something, doesn't it?" I asked. Nancy didn't reply. She didn't need to.

And so, after nearly two centuries, the terrible secret of Ferry Street came to light—a final note on the tragedy.

Except for a long-forsaken lover who still comes knocking at the door.

## ESTHER'S PLAYFUL ESCAPADES

Martine's is a small inn run by a charming gal named Martine Landry whose restaurant and bar are among New Hope's most popular. In the late eighteenth century, the house was built as a toll house for the ferry that carried passengers across the Delaware. For many years, the pulley-shaped wheel that was used to haul in the ferry boats could be seen upstairs in the inn, hanging high on the wall. In 1798, the old building also operated as a salt house. (This was in the time before refrigeration when salt was used to preserve food.)

In the twentieth century, the building served mainly as the village public library. In fact, I researched up there many a day in my writing career. One of the most dedicated and best-loved librarians was a woman named Esther. She was gentle and concerned and always eager to help those who came in. According to many individuals who work here now, and worked here in the past, Esther still labors devotedly on the premises!

Take, for example, the experience of Lisa Jefferson. She told of the many times she'd come into the inn in the mornings and descend into the cellar to gather supplies. Almost always when she did so, Esther would be there. Not a clearly-defined form but a shadow-like shape looking at Lisa from one side. Lisa was a bit unnerved at first but eventually she came to feel the presence was gentle and good and she ceased to feel afraid.

A young girl named Wendy, whose aunt once owned the inn said one night after closing up, she started down the street and looked back over one shoulder. She looked up, and in the lamp light, was startled to see a woman standing in the second story window. She was small and waifish with gray hair and a sweet expression on her face.

*Esther, who at one time served as the town librarian, still haunts her former place of employment: the historic toll house building located at Main and Ferry Streets in New Hope.*

Jennifer Roberts, who was working at the inn back in the 1970s when it was then called "The Picnic Basket," recalls sitting at the bar downstairs on a particularly slow night with another co-worker, Bert Rescenske. "There was no business that evening, so the two of us were sitting there debating whether to close up early and call it a night. Dinner service was over and the upstairs dining room was all tidied up for the next day. All of a sudden, the two of us heard a noise coming from upstairs. We looked at each other and laughed... 'Must be Esther.' We went upstairs to investigate and saw that all of the chairs that we had turned over on top of the tables were now on the floor and scattered about. Bert and I looked at each other and said without hesitation—'Time to close.'"

Chrissie Clawson who was a bartender at Martine's for many years, also told me about her close encounters with Esther. One Saturday night during the summertime, Chrissie was working the late night shift. Before closing up the inn, she checked to make sure that everything was in order. The basement door had to be closed tight since the ice machine was located down there. (This was particularly important in the summer months so that the basement area would remain as cool as possible.) She tidied up the bar and then checked the upstairs dining area to make sure that all of the tables had been reset for lunch. She locked up the inn and then went home to catch a few hours of sleep before she had to report back to work at 7:00 a.m. the next morning. "When I walked in that morning, I noticed that the speed rack behind the bar (which stored all of the major liquors and mixers) had been picked up and was on the floor. Then I noticed that the basement door was wide open. When I checked the upstairs dining room, guess what? All of the silverware on the tables had been rearranged. I thought to myself, 'Wow. This time she really did it. Esther's hit all three floors!' Since I knew that I was the last one to leave the night before and the first one in that morning, there was no other explanation for all of this mischievous activity other than good ol' Esther!"

More recently, a waiter tells of a party in the inn that was interrupted by a sudden black out. There seemed to be no cause. No storm. No overloaded circuits. Just sudden darkness. But no one got upset. The party continued in darkness until the lights could be turned on again. It just seemed to be a general agreement that Esther liked the merriment and fun and was eager to have her presence be known.

Old-time residents say Esther was just like that in life. She enjoyed seeing others happy. Perhaps, her playful antics are just a way of letting everyone know that she is pleased with the new life that has come to the old library building.

\*

*Martine's Restaurant has now moved to 14 E. Ferry Street where patrons can enjoy riverside dining. The original toll house building at 7 Ferry Street is now occupied by a new restaurant. The site continues to be Esther's playful, haunting grounds.*

# "LIZA MINNELLI" PAYS A VISIT

Driving up Ferry Street, just past the railroad tracks, there was a charming lavender house with a black wrought-iron, front-yard gate. It was owned by a good friend of mine, Tom Lynch. At the time he was living here, Tom also operated a gift shop on Mechanic Street called The Cheshire Cat. The ghosts at his shop were more than could be counted, but he also experienced a visit from the Spirit World at his Ferry Street home.

Tom once had a very dear and close friend—an artist. She and her husband used to come to New Hope frequently to visit Tom. Then one summer, Tom noticed that Jean looked unusually thin and pale. He soon learned that she had been diagnosed with cancer. This was terrible news to Tom. He was absolutely devastated.

*Jean Burnbaum and Tom Lynch shared a close friendship for many years.*

One day, a few months later, Tom was working at the shop and for some unexplainable reason he started to feel so exhausted that he could hardly stand up. He told his assistant that he was going home to bed.

He came home. The clock struck three as he dragged himself up the stairway inside. Suddenly he was startled by a loud, shattering sound. He turned and could hardly believe his eyes. The hall window—the whole pane—for no reason at all had sharply cracked! The incident was terribly shaking. Later Tom knew why it had happened. He got a phone call from Jean's husband in New York. She had taken her life at three-o-clock that afternoon.

Tom went to bed sick at heart that night. He was shocked and sad and grief-stricken. Then in the darkness he suddenly awakened. There had been a movement in the room and the sound aroused him from his restless sleep. As he listened alertly, he felt the side of his bed slowly sink from the weight of someone sitting on it. He snapped on the light. "At first glance I thought it was Liza Minnelli sitting on the edge of my bed," said Tom. But, seconds later, he realized that it was Jean who was seated there. He was a little taken aback by her outfit. She was clothed utterly differently from the way she dressed in actual life, Tom said. She had on gold dangle earrings, a jazzy knit top, tight-fitting pants and stiletto heels.

Tom sat bolt upright in surprise.

"Hi, Tom!" she said, as she crossed her legs, "I know you are feeling bad about what happened but you really mustn't. I did the right thing. And taking pills is such an easy way. Of course, Nate is troubled. He would be. This whole thing is going to be hard for him to handle. But don't you be concerned. Please don't worry, Tom. I feel just great."

With that, the friend vanished and Tom found himself alone in his bedroom.

Jean came again to Tom, in the same way, saying pretty much the same things for the next three nights. Finally, Tom turned to his friend and said "Jean, you've got to stop doing this! I'm not getting any sleep!" That was it. He never saw her again. No more visits. Tom felt she didn't have to return. He came to honor her choice and accept what she did. It started to make sense to him and gradually his grief dissipated. Tom feels certain that Jean is now happy where she is.

A scene in Venice, which Jean painted for Tom used to hang on one of the shop walls at the Cheshire Cat. With just one glance, Tom could be transported to a world of splendor and enchantment, a haven of tranquility. He likes to think that Jean is part of that same world, too.

# The Luck of the Logan

*The Logan Inn, built 5 years before George Washington was born, stands in the heart of New Hope. Room Six is considered to be the "hot spot" for paranormal activity.*

The Logan Inn is one of the five oldest inns in the United States. Located in the heart of New Hope, it was originally established as a tavern in 1727. During the Revolutionary War, Washington and his men reportedly stopped by to seek sustenance and shelter. It should come as no surprise that throughout the passing centuries this historic old building has accumulated quite a number of ghosts and specters. It is reputed to be one of the most haunted buildings in all of New Hope.

As the years have gone by, the inn has changed hands from one proprietor to another, but the ghosts remain.

In the 1970s a gentleman by the name of Carl Lutz bought the inn. He embraced the presence of all the Other World residents that dwelled within the establishment. "There's nothing to be afraid of," he used to say. "All of our ghosts are benevolent. I believe some of them are here to actually protect the Logan Inn."

Revolutionary soldiers have been seen wandering the inn. A little girl has been known to greet visitors in the parking lot. The strong fragrance of lavender has been detected wafting throughout the hallway as guests pass by the portrait of Carl's grandparents. (His grandmother, Elizabeth, adored lavender perfume.) Perhaps, the most haunted spot in the whole inn is Room Six. Pillows get tugged and tossed, lights flick on and off. Footsteps and voices are heard. The face of a man appears from time to time in the bathroom mirror. Some guests have reported seeing a white, misty shape swirling around the room.

One day when I stopped by the Logan Inn to chat with Carl, he told me of another unusual incident that had taken place in the building. Apparently, he had gone down into the basement to fetch some supplies and suddenly a beautiful, peach-colored, glass globe glimmered back up at him from the dirt floor. He carefully picked it up and took it upstairs and put it on display in a little cabinet behind the bar. And then he told me one day it vanished. He came down in the morning and it was gone. Years passed by, and there was no sign of the glass ball. And then one day, it reappeared! Carl walked into the tavern room and there it was, back on display in the cabinet behind the bar.

The witch ball is a very fascinating part of witchcraft lore. For centuries it was believed to be a good way to keep the evil eye out of your home. The people both in England and in this country would hang a witch ball in a net or stand it on a pedestal near a window or door. There were different kinds of balls used to insure protection against evil spirits, negativity, sickness or ill fortune. In England, the silvered mirror type was very popular as the theory was that if the evil eye tried to get in, it would reflect back on the witch and she would suffer from it—not the household members. Others believed that the witch would be so entranced with her own reflection in the silver mirrored ball that she would stare at herself until morning and then have to fly away when the sun came up.

The witch ball found at the Logan Inn is quite unique. It is a glass orb of swirling peach colors with a small hole in one end. Before I researched witchcraft lore, I always wondered what the purpose was for that small opening. It was so tiny that it appeared to serve

*An antique witch ball, made of finely spun glass, has been known to mysteriously disappear and reappear at the Logan Inn.*

no function. Finally, I found an explanation for this particular kind of spirit ball. Apparently, people believed that the spinning colors would first mesmerize the evil spirit and draw it toward the ball. Once drawn to the ball, the spirit would the fly into the hole and become trapped within the intricate webbings of glass strands. This would prevent the spirit from affecting its surroundings.

Today glass witch balls are displayed as works of art, beautiful decorations or, perhaps, just as a fun conversation piece. Carl Lutz believed his spirit ball was a "Globe of Good Fortune." Since most antique witches balls were either blue or green, the peach color of this particular orb makes it even more unique. "Peach is the color that symbolizes strength, protection, fascination and attraction," he told me. "It's considered the Luck of the Logan."

Beautiful to look at, powerfully protective... stop by the Logan Inn and take a look at this mysterious object for yourself.

*The Logan Inn is listed on the National Registry of Historic Places. The current owners, Pete and Nick Gialias, completed an extensive renovation that preserved the charm and craftsmanship of the original building along with the addition of modern amenities. The witch ball remains on display behind the tavern bar.*

## STAGE FRIGHT

In the heart of New Hope, stands the famous Bucks County Playhouse built from the old Parry Grist Mill. As everyone knows, its walls and floorboards have reverberated to the voices and footsteps of hundreds of luminaries since it was erected in the 1930s, but few people know that these walls have also encased some unearthly doings.

For one thing, the costume changing area below, over by the dam, is said to be the habitat of spirits from the past. Several people who are closely associated with the Playhouse have no doubt that "shadow-walkers" like to gather there. Many of them have told me there is definitely a feeling of a strange and haunting presence down in that old area which is part of the original grist mill.

Not so long ago the musical director there at the time, Newton Gilchrist, told me the same thing. "There is unquestionably a presence down in that old storage area. I have felt it many times." Most unsettling of all though, to the entire cast of one performance, was an eerie experience back in 1978 when the group was putting on the show *Music Man*. Newton was in the musical himself and still vividly recalls the incident.

"It was during the second act and the entire cast was on stage," he recalled to me. "We were taking our places on a bridge getting ready for the marvelous parade scene. It was a moment of transition. No one was singing at the time but, suddenly, a strong, high pitched scream resounded throughout the theater. We were rocked. It sounded like a cry of agony. The producer hastily rushed upstairs thinking that a prankster must have somehow hijacked the sound box. He was stunned to find the room completely empty."

I wondered to myself, could it have been a call from beyond? Did

*In 1939, an old gristmill located in the center of town was transformed into the Bucks County Playhouse. For decades, the theater has been the site of many unexplained psychic occurrences.*

any traumatic event occur in connection with the Playhouse in the past that could have caused such a disturbing interruption? Was it a voice from an unhappy situation that had once occurred?

I found that there had been one such incident.

In 1966, the *Lion in Winter* was playing here with George C. Scott in the leading role of King Henry II. Scott's wife, Colleen Dewhurst, played the female lead, Queen Eleanor. The supporting role of Philip, King of France, was played by a handsome, young actor by the name of Richard Lynch, who unfortunately, was not able to live up to the professional standards of his associates. He persistently came on stage stoned out of his mind.

Although Richard was warned by his fellow actors and the director, and everyone else that he needed to "clean up his act," he seemed unable to heed their advice. Repeatedly, he missed his cues and would stumble onto the stage inebriated or tripped out on drugs. More than once, he interrupted the action of the play with some kind of slurring dialogue or nonsensical muttering. One night,

Scott was in the middle of his most important monologue in the entire play; "*My life when it is written will read better than it lived...*" when all of a sudden the young, wasted actor staggered out on the stage interrupting him. George C. managed to ad lib his way through the speech, but after the show, he grabbed the youth by his collar and yelled, "You goddamned SOB! If you ever do that to me on stage again, I'll kill you!"

The actor, obviously a disturbed young man, went back to New York and a few months later did the unthinkable—he walked into Central Park one day at high noon under the influence of LSD, doused himself with kerosene, and lit a match! Amazingly enough, he did not die. He was rescued before he burned himself to death. But the results were dire nevertheless. He face was permanently deformed and his facial expressions were rendered immobile by the scars from his severe burns. Never again would Richard Lynch stride across the stage as the handsome, blonde hero with a strong, gaunt face.

So the question remains, did Lynch return in revengeful thought over a decade later to the place that continued to haunt his memory? Did his angry, self-destructive energy still remain in the Playhouse atmosphere? Was the jubilant, grand finale scene of "Seventy-six Trombones" preceded by a shriek from the past, an omen from a young, crazed actor still burning with fury and madness?

*

*After nearly killing himself in 1967, Richard Lynch put an end to his drinking and drug addiction. He successfully resurrected his acting career and has starred in film and television for over 20 years. He is best known for playing villains. His distinctly scarred appearance is perfectly suited to the role of evil characters.*

## CHEWY'S MOURNFUL CHANT

Many years ago, Jessica Savitch was one of the most recognized news personalities in America. She was known as the "Golden Girl of TV" and the "Goddess of NBC." She was bright and beautiful, poised and plucky, sassy and classy and above all, she was ambitious. This young woman had an unstoppable drive to make it to the top in the world of broadcasting journalism. In the early 1970s, female reporters were a rarity. In fact, a professor at Ithaca College had advised Jessica to seek another career path telling her "There's no room for broads in broadcasting." But that didn't stop Jessica. She was determined to break into this male-dominated business and make a name for herself. And she did. She worked obsessively, sacrificing her own personal happiness to her career. By the time she was thirty years old, she had finally reached her goal. She was given the job as news anchor for NBC Nightly News along with hosting the Prime Time show on Sunday.

All of this hard work exacted a heavy toll on Jessica. Unbeknownst to the thousands of television viewers and fans who adored her, she was besieged with many troubles, struggles and secrets. But, none of this was evident to the outside world. Jessica Savitch had that mysterious air of stardom about her. When she flashed her trademark smile at the end of every news report, the audience was smitten. Behind this beautiful blonde façade, however, there existed quite a lonely, fragile, and insecure young lady who was fighting with all her might to make it in a man's world. She used to adorn herself with a gold "#1" necklace, but close friends who knew her well said that Jessica was always filled with self-doubt.

For years, she was involved in an on-again, off-again, love-hate relationship with a fellow television newsman named Ron Kershaw. It was an abusive, dysfunctional, complicated, and emotionally charged love affair. They couldn't live with each other and they couldn't live without each other. After one of their many break-ups, Ron gave her a Siberian Husky pup named Chewy. It didn't take long for this friendly, energetic, female puppy (who liked to chew up everything in sight) to become Jessica's favorite and constant companion. She absolutely doted on the dog. Chewy could do no wrong. Wherever Jessica went, Chewy went. She even took the pup to work.

It's easy to understand her instant attachment to this dog. By the time Chewy arrived in Jessica's life, she had gone through two failed marriages. She divorced her first husband after just ten months of marriage. Shortly thereafter, she married again but this relationship was also doomed. Less than five months later her second husband committed suicide. Although Ron Kershaw always remained the most important man in her life, they were never able to break free from the frenzied, destructive pattern of their relationship.

And then along came Chewy. It's no wonder that this loveable, blue-eyed furry creature seemed to be the answer to all of Jessica's emotional needs. She could pour all of her affection into Chewy without any fear of disappointment, conflict, abuse, or competition. And what did she get in return? It's my guess that Chewy really did consider Jessica to be "#1!"

In spite of all of her professional success and accomplishments, Jessica continued to fight her own inner demons. There were ongoing rumors of her cocaine addiction, her dependence on Valium and painkillers, and her anorexic disorder. From time to time she found herself haunted by the early death of her father. In fact, she used to have premonitions about her own death telling friends that she didn't think she would live much longer than her father. Her deep unhappiness, coupled with her anxiety about the future, prompted her to contact a psychic. She often consulted with Joan Durham (a well known psychic who lives in New Jersey), as a way to ease her fears.

In mid-October of 1983, Jessica was making every effort to pick up the pieces of her life. After a disastrous live newscast on October 3, in which she stumbled and slurred over her words and gave a totally bizarre performance, she knew she had hit rock bottom. Her credibility as a news broadcaster was shattered in just

43 seconds. Nevertheless, Jessica was determined to hang in there. She would fight back with every ounce of pluck and courage to regain her status as "The Unflappable Queen of TV." Besides, she now had a new love interest who seemed intelligent, interesting, and most of all, stable. So at least something was going right in her life.

Martin Fischbein was the Vice President of the New York Post. They had been dating for several weeks and the relationship seemed to be working. Jessica appeared to be happy and light-hearted. They enjoyed going to the theater, dining out, and taking walks through the park with Chewy. With all the fun they were having together, she decided they should try something else—an escapade to Bucks County, Pennsylvania, a place that she had always loved. Jessica suggested that they take a trip to New Hope. She was convinced that Martin would love the area as much as she did

They planned the trip for Sunday, October 23, hoping it would be a beautiful autumn day. Unfortunately, the weather did not cooperate. They left New York City in a downpour of rain. Martin had rented an Oldsmobile Cutlass Cruiser so that there would be plenty of room for Chewy in the back of the car. The three of them piled into the blue station wagon, and with the windshield wipers at full speed, they headed towards New Hope.

In spite of the rain, they spent a leisurely afternoon poking through shops, admiring antiques, visiting galleries and stopping for some hot coffee. They had made a booking in advance to have dinner at one of Jessica's favorite restaurants in the area, Chez Odette's. Due to the inclement weather, the couple decided to change their 6:30 p.m. reservation to an hour earlier. They were eager to get out of the rain and enjoy some delicious French food by the warmth of a fireplace. Though Odette was long gone from her familiar position as starring hostess in her charming restaurant and cabaret, the two of them were, no doubt, warmly greeted as Jessica was famous herself for being one of Philadelphia's most popular TV personalities.

The restaurant turned out to be a cozy refuge from the storm. The fireside table in the rustic bar room provided the perfect ambience for the hungry, rain-soaked couple. Although Jessica was looking forward to enjoying a good meal with her new beau, she was also very nervous about leaving her beloved dog all alone in the car. The storm was getting progressively worse and she was worried about how Chewy might react to the thunder and lightening.

*The site where Jessica Savitch, her beau, and her beloved dog, drowned in October, 1983, after their car overturned into a section of the Delaware Canal. Presently, the canal remains devoid of water and overgrown with natural debris until all flood repairs have been completed.*

They gave the waiter their food order as soon as they could. After finishing their meal a little after 7:00 p.m., the two of them left the restaurant in an absolute downpour of rain. As soon as they got to the car, Jessica climbed into the back seat to check on Chewy. No doubt, she felt her dog needed to be soothed and comforted. Martin strapped himself into the driver's seat, started the engine, turned on the headlights, and got the wipers going at top speed. He backed the car out of the parking space cautiously, and then without knowing it, Martin Fischbein made a fateful mistake. Instead of proceeding towards the proper exit of the parking lot, he turned on to the dirt towpath that borders the old Delaware Canal. We can only assume that due to the onslaught of rain he was unable to see the "No Outlet" signs that were posted there. The station wagon veered to the left, flipped over the edge of the canal, and then plunged down 15 ft. into the shallow water.

Soon the car began to sink into deep mud which sealed up the doors. Martin and Jessica were trapped inside as the water poured in.

Around 11:30 p.m. that night John Nyari, who owned Odette's at the time and also had a house right next to the tow path, discovered the wreck. Within minutes, the New Hope police and the Lambertville Rescue Squad arrived at the scene of the accident. The rescuers discovered Martin's body still strapped behind the wheel. They believe that he had been knocked unconscious when the car overturned. Jessica's body was found in the back seat. It was obvious that she had struggled with every ounce of her being to escape. Autopsies on the bodies were done at Doylestown Hospital. "Death by asphyxiation" was the final ruling. According to police reports, drugs and alcohol played no part in the crash. It was simply a tragic accident.

At 1:00 a.m. that morning, news of what had happened reached the wire services at NBC. Jessica Savitch, one of the most recognized news personalities in America, was now the subject of the day's leading headlines. The Golden Girl of TV was dead at 36 years of age.

And what happened to Chewy?

Somehow Chewy's body ended up being thrown down by the side of the canal. It had been reported that some of the rescue workers mistook the dog's body for a fur coat. When Ron Kershaw appeared at the scene of the accident (he left Baltimore in a flash and drove up to New Hope as soon as he heard the news), he immediately identified, and rescued the body of Jessica's beloved pet. The Savitch family decided that Jessica and her faithful companion, Chewy, would be cremated together. Two days later, after a brief memorial service in Atlantic City, their ashes were scattered together in the stormy Atlantic Ocean.

When I heard about this tragic incident myself, I had no doubt that such a heartbreaking story would end here. Although a sign had been posted at the edge of the towpath stating "ALL DOGS MUST BE ON LEASH," there have been numerous sightings of a dog that is *not* on a leash. Over the years, I have heard reports about a "phantom dog" seen running down the towpath late at night with its white-tipped sickle tail brushing the air. Some people have stopped to see if the animal is lost but when they approach the dog, it just disappears. On a few occasions, a dog has been seen on the grassy area right near the very spot where Jessica and Chewy took their very last breath together.

A mournful howl has been known to pierce the silence of the darkest night.

*

*In the book, Golden Girl: The Story of Jessica Savitch, by Alanna Nash, the author reported that in June, 1983, Jessica Savitch had a reading with her psychic, Joan Durham. In this meeting, Durham warned her about "problems with driving." She said she saw a "dark blue car with a shattered windshield and the face of a blonde woman pressed up against it." Joan Durham, was the medium my mother hired to conduct one of her most popular ghost tours called "Supper and a Séance." Durham has been named as one of the top psychics in America.*

## A NOTE TO READERS

I have taken the liberty of adding two more stories to this Haunted Village section. John Byers, Geri Delevich, and Lucianne DiLeo, all long-time residents of New Hope, never had the opportunity to share their ghostly experiences with my mother, but they did have a chance to tell me.

*Lynda Elizabeth Jeffrey*

## VALENTINE BROKE HER HEART

John Byers is currently the owner and proprietor of Porches on the Towpath, a charming Bed and Breakfast located in the heart of New Hope. John first arrived in the Bucks County region when he was a young man in his early 20s. He was eager to settle down and establish himself in an area that would stimulate his creative talents. He loved gardening, landscaping, renovating, and decorating. With a small sum of inherited money, John purchased some run-down houses in Lambertville, New Jersey, set about fixing them up, and then, in no time at all, resold them for a considerable profit. Byers, a natural entrepreneur, went on to get his real estate license and quickly made a name for himself as a smart, savvy, and hard-working businessman.

In the early 1970s, John and his partner, Bernard Robin, purchased a large piece of property on Upper York Road that had been left in an estate. The property had been on the market for a considerable amount of time. "One day I was driving into Solebury Village and spotted an old farmhouse that was tucked behind a fieldstone perimeter wall, very close to the intersection of Route 263 and North Sugan Road," said John. "For some reason I can't even explain, I just connected to it. I kept going back to the house over and over again. Before we had even made an offer, I had drawn up plans for the garden and the pond."

Byers and Robin got the house, moved in, and began working their "magic" on it. "We didn't have a lot of renovations to do, but we did make one significant change," John told me. "We decided to take out the back staircase that ran between the first floor and one of the upstairs bedrooms. That way we could carve out enough space for a powder room on the main floor. We also contacted Holicong Central Security to install an alarm system for us. Since the house stood on twenty-eight acres of ground and was in the middle of nowhere, we thought it was a good idea to have some additional protection."

No sooner had the house been wired for security when John and Bernard began experiencing a real hassle with the alarm system. "The darn thing kept going off for no reason," said John. "We'd call Holicong, and they'd come out to the house to inspect the system and time after time, they'd tell us the same thing. 'It's not the system. You guys must be doing something wrong.' We would shake our heads emphatically and say over and over again, 'It's not us. We know that."

So the question remained, what the heck was tripping off the alarm system?

John and Bernard were totally baffled by what was going on in their house.

"It was hard for us to get any sleep," John continued. "We would go to bed and then in the dead of night we'd be awakened by the shrill sound of a 'Beep, Beep, Beep.' The first time this happened, I remember jumping out of bed immediately. I stepped into the hallway and noticed that the door of an adjacent bedroom was wide open. That was somewhat frightening since I knew for a fact that I had not only closed that door before going to bed but I had locked it as well."

John went on to explain to me that all doors in an old house open "in," but this particular door opened "out." "I distinctly remember locking the door. I saw the tongue slide over. The door was locked. I have no doubt about that."

The room had been a focus of the renovation, John said. "I wondered if there was a former occupant who was mad at us for removing the rear staircase? Were they coming back to let us know of their displeasure?"

This same disturbing nightly routine continued on and off again for several months.

*John Byers felt the ghostly presence of a lonely woman who came back to haunt her former place of residence.*

John continued, "One day, I said to myself, 'Okay, enough is enough.' I decided to reprimand our invisible guest. I just spelled it out clearly. 'Look, if you're going to open the bedroom door and wander around our house late at night, this is the path you need to take in order not to trip off the alarm system. Watch me.' I then proceeded to demonstrate how it was possible to avoid the sensor by going down the stairs in a particular manner and by making a tight turn around the stair post.

"Guess what? It worked! Occasionally, we would still find the bedroom door left open, but we never had a problem with the alarm going off."

"So, did you ever figure out what was going on?" I asked.

"Yep, I did," said John.

He then went on to tell me exactly who he thought the ghost was. The more he talked, the more it became apparent to me why John's unknown visitor had come back to haunt the house that he and his partner were now living in.

Yes, it was *her* house at one time… but there's more to the story than just that.

Way back in the 1930s, a wealthy doctor named Dr. Hawkins purchased the old farm house and the miles of acreage that surrounded it. He renovated the place and quickly turned it into a country homestead for his family as well as for his medical practice. He lived in the house for decades with his daughter, Genevieve.

As a young woman, Genevieve Hawkins fell madly in love with a well known stained glass artist, Valentine D'Ogries, who lived in the nearby area. Val was born in Austria, but eventually came to the states. At the age of 36 he opened up an art studio in Carversville, a small rural town quite close to where the Hawkins family was living in Solebury Village. Val achieved a great deal of fame as a noted ecclesiastical artist. Even today, his murals, frescoes, altarpieces and stained glass windows grace many of the most beautiful churches in America.

Unfortunately, Genevieve's love was not reciprocated. Val D'Ogries had absolutely no interest in her. He was a gay man.

Genevieve spent her whole life pining away for him. Eventually, she inherited the house and property from her father, but she lived there all alone. She never married. It would be Val or no one. She did keep herself busy working on the estate, peddling her fresh farm eggs, and at one time she even assumed the role of Solebury's Postmaster. Genevieve obviously felt an attachment to this small rural community. She eventually bequeathed a large amount of acreage to the local school.

This lonely woman, whom the locals nicknamed "The Egg Lady," seemed to live such an empty and sad life. Everyone who knew her said that she was forever haunted by her unrequited love for Valentine.

Walking around the property one day, John happened to discover a strange, tell-tale sign of Genevieve's deep unhappiness. As he was strolling through the hedgerow, he noticed a carving on the trunk of a beech tree. He looked closely and saw a distinct message

*Valetine D'Ogries (1889-1959) created these two stained glass panels for St. Philip's Chapel in New Hope, Pa.*

chiseled out on the side of the tree. First, the word "Genevieve" and then below her name, the outline of a heart, and then below the carved heart there was nothing but a deep gash. "It looked like a blackened scar," John said. "I stared at the slash and thought to myself, 'That really says it all.'"

Of course, by the time John saw the carving on the tree trunk, he had already heard the story about Genevieve and her ill-fated love. "It's so sad. She tortured herself by falling in love with a man who could never love her back."

I listened carefully as John related all of these bizarre events to me. "Not so strange," I thought to myself. It made perfect sense to me that Genevieve would come back to haunt her old domicile while John and Bernard were living there.

Even though it was many years later, I think the house still retained the heavy sadness and emotional loss that came from her devastating, one-sided love affair. Although Genevieve had died, I believe the energy of her unfulfilled longings and desires hovered over the abode and became activated by the presence of two young, gay men, both of whom were handsome, charming, sensitive, and artistic. It's my guess that subconsciously John must have felt a rapport with this despondent woman and her love story.

John and Bernard sold the house a couple of years later and said farewell to the Spinster of Sugan Road.

I'm wondering... did the two of them break Genevieve's heart as well?

*

*Valentine D'Ogries created two stained glass panels to flank the front doors of St. Philip's Chapel in New Hope, Pennsylvania. This small, charming Episcopal church occupies an old stone building that was once a one-room school house. D'Ogries also presented the church with color drawings for other stained glass windows that he had designed.*

## A GHOST NAMED MARGARET

Everyone in New Hope knows Geri Delevich. She's been a high profile person in town ever since 1976 when she moved into a rambling, old, wooden-frame house located just across the street from the historic flax mills on Old Mill Road.

Geri was an elementary school teacher for 33 years, winning numerous awards for her visionary ideas and her innovative techniques. She has dedicated herself to the New Hope community, serving as a borough councilwoman for over a decade, and working hard to project the town's image as not only an appealing tourist destination, but also as a place that embraces differences. "Everyone feels at home here. It doesn't matter who you are. New Hope is about freedom, acceptance, respect for one another, and living together in harmony."

Geri is the first to admit that many ghosts must feel the same way about the town. "It's clear that this 'haunted village' embraces its invisible residents and visitors with the same degree of acceptance and approval that it holds out to everyone else. We all love New Hope," says Delevich, "and that includes those of us in the real world as well as those beings who have come back from the Spirit World."

The first night that Geri moved into her century-old home on Old Mill Road she believes she received a brief message from some unknown spirit. "I went to bed that night exhausted from the move and fell into a deep sleep. All of a sudden, I woke up. I felt a motion, as if someone sat down on the end of the bed. Then I heard a voice that uttered simply one word, 'TURN.' I was totally startled. I knew there was no one else in the room with me. It was the strangest thing. I stayed in bed without moving a muscle trying to figure out what the meaning of this word could be."

Ever since that night Geri has been mulling over the various possibilities of what "turn" might have signified. "I still don't know," she said. "Perhaps it was a reference to the fact that this recent move would *turn* my life around in a new direction? Sometimes I think the voice may have said 'RETURN.' I have often wondered if I might have lived in this house in another lifetime. Perhaps, that first night I stayed here someone was trying to tell me that it was time to *return* home?"

To this day, Geri still hasn't settled on a clear-cut answer as to what that voice in the dark was trying to tell her.

Even before Delevich moved in, the house had a history of strange things happening.

At one time, Lucianne DiLeo decided to take up residence in the old home with a friend of hers who had two children. They wanted to spruce up the place so they hired an interior painter to put a fresh coat of paint on all the walls. Lucianne and her friend looked over a large array of paint samples and agreed upon a specific color for each room in the house. The kids got to pick out the colors for their rooms too. When the house painter arrived and began scraping the walls, they were amazed to discover that the new paint colors they had selected for every room were an exact match to the original colors. "We couldn't believe it," said Lucianne. "It was really eerie because we had picked out such odd colors. Without knowing it, we were obviously 'in tune' with the original color scheme. How weird is that?"

It seems to me that they must have felt such a connection to this old home that, subconsciously, they were drawn to the identical shades and tones that reflected the history of the house.

Unfortunately, their dog did not feel that same kind of positive connection. From the moment they moved into the house, they noticed a distinct change in their animal's behavior. April was normally a quiet dog but now they would hear her barking non-stop at what appeared to be absolutely nothing. The dog seemed to become easily agitated and frenzied. She even started biting the children. As much as they tried, they were unable to get their four-legged friend to settle down. The growling, gnawing, and biting continued.

Out of concern for the children, they finally decided to take April to the SPCA in Lahaska. They explained that the dog had now become an "unwanted animal." They told the truth about her sudden change of temperament and the recent attacks they had experienced. They even suggested that the dog be put to sleep rather than put up for adoption. It wasn't long before they got a call from one of the volunteers at the shelter. "We just want you to know that April has been here for a whole week and has been nothing but friendly, sweet and affectionate. We see no reason to euthanize this dog. She will make a great pet for some lucky person."

They were stunned. What was going on? Had the dog sensed a presence in the house on Old Mill Road that they were not aware of? Perhaps the family pet saw something, or someone, in the house that the rest of the occupants could not see.

Lucianne also spoke of a "blanket of silence" that would suddenly fall over the house. "It was so strange. In the middle of a busy day, the house would suddenly be enveloped in a feeling of hushed stillness. The only thing I can compare it to is the quietness of the first winter snowfall."

One night, Lucianne was alone in the house when she was awakened by an odd sound. She sat up in bed and listened closely. Was it the ice maker, or perhaps hailstones hitting the roof of the house? It was a rhythmic sound going "click-click, click-click," over and over again. Although she was a bit frightened, she decided to get up and investigate. Roaming from one room to another, she followed the echoes of the sound until she got to the kitchen. What do you suppose she found? There on the kitchen counter was a handful of marbles! Now, these were no ordinary marbles. Years ago, Lucianne had purchased a jar of antique marbles. They were handmade, clay marbles that dated back to the Revolutionary War era. She had decided to display the two dozen old marbles in a glass canister with a lid on it. She kept the jar of marbles on her kitchen counter. It was a wonderful conversation piece.

But that night she found the marbles out of the jar and spread out in a precise crescent shape on her kitchen counter top. She could not explain this midnight disturbance.

*One night, a playful ghost decided to leave a surprise for Lucianne DiLeo on her kitchen countertop.*

Another item on display in the house is a Revolutionary War cannon ball which Lucianne came across accidentally when she was out digging in the garden years ago. She took the heavy-weighted, round ball to the Mercer Museum. It was authenticated as a cannon ball that was used in Revolutionary times. Fortunately, no playful spirits have decided to mess around with the 5.5 lb. cannon ball (at least, not yet), but it does seem like they wanted to have a little fun shooting marbles late one night.

When Geri moved in, she also sensed a strong presence that seemed to hover over the house. But it wasn't a frightening spirit. She decided that the unknown visitor would have to fit the image she had in mind if it wanted to remain in her house. "I couldn't bear the thought that it might be the spirit of a Revolutionary soldier who had died at a young age. I couldn't live with that. So I decided that if I was going to share my house with a ghost it would have to be a nice woman that I could live with! I settled on a female spirit and I gave her the name, Margaret."

Geri and Lucianne had come to learn that one of the former occupants of the house was named Margaret. At the time she lived there, she wore a brace on her leg. Since one of the ghostly manifestations in the house was the sound of an unusual gait along with the resonance of a "dragging" sound, it seemed reasonable to imagine that Margaret still liked hanging around her old home.

Margaret appeared to be friendly and funny and more of a mischief-maker than anything else. She was into playing pranks and creating a little amusement and diversion. Or perhaps I should say, she was one of those specters who was always looking for a good time.

When Geri told me this story, I couldn't help but smile at Margaret's cleverness and coordination in pulling off a little tomfoolery in the house. "One day I couldn't find my watch," said Geri. "When I take the watch off at night, I'm very habitual. I always put it in the same place. I've never deviated from this routine. But, lo and behold, this time my watch was missing! I looked high and low. No watch. I continued searching for it, but had no success. Then I explained to Margaret that my parents had given me the watch. I wanted her to know that I was very sentimentally attached to it. In spite of my pleading, nothing turned up for several days. Finally, I just got mad. I shouted out 'Okay, Margaret, I want my watch back!' The next morning, I went into the kitchen and opened up the cabinet to get out a juice glass, another one of my habitual routines which I performed every morning. Much to my surprise, there was my watch. It was right in front of the line of glasses that we had stored in the cabinet.

"And, that wasn't the end of it. I happened to notice that my bedroom clock was unplugged. I kneeled down, put the plug back into the wall, and then proceeded to go about my business. A few minutes later, I glanced at the clock and noticed that it still wasn't working. Oh, no. Margaret's at it again! I got a flashlight and reached under the bed for the long extension cord that I had connected to the end cord of the clock. You guessed it—someone had pulled out the plug from the extension cord that was underneath my bed. At that moment I also discovered something else that was kinda spooky. My bedroom clock and my missing wrist watch had both stopped at precisely the same time. I knew this was not just a 'coincidence.' This was definitely the work of our gal, Margaret."

At this point, Geri and Lucianne discussed what they might do about "Margaret." Lucianne was taking courses at Villanova and one of her psychology teachers knew an associate (a professor at the University of Pennsylvania) who had a keen interest in the paranormal. He liked to think of himself as a real "ghost hunter." This gentleman offered to come to their house and conduct a séance. He said that he would bring along his camera, too. He was hoping to capture some orbs on film.

"We decided to check with Margaret first," said Geri.

"One night Lucianne and I sat quietly in the living room and focused our thoughts on this playful, invisible friend of ours that we had come to know so well.

"We talked to her just like she was our good buddy. We asked her point blank... 'Margaret, would you like us to hold a séance in your honor? We don't want to disturb you so let us know what you would like.'

"We know that spirits are sensitive," said Geri, "so we spoke to her with great sincerity and a lot of empathy. I wanted Margaret to know that we were supportive and understanding. We told her that we could feel her restlessness and pain.

"We repeated over and over again, 'It's okay, Margaret. You can leave this place. We release you from this world. Go in peace.'

"After our heart-to-heart talk with Margaret, we got the distinct feeling that she did not want us to call in a medium or make any concentrated efforts to contact her again. We felt like we had released her with love and compassion to go on to the Other World."

There was never another sign of Margaret.

"I must admit, we were a little disappointed to have her go. My nieces and nephews liked to come over and see if Margaret would try and pull any fast tricks on them, but in the end I think it worked out as it should. Margaret knew that we cared about her. We were never afraid of her, in fact, we actually felt sorry for her."

Geri is one of the most caring and kind-hearted individuals that I know.

It doesn't surprise me that she was the one who was finally able to convince Margaret that it was time to "Go in peace."

# PEERING INTO THE FUTURE

Intuition comes very close to clairvoyance;
it appears to be the extrasensory perception of reality.

*

*Alexis Carrel*

# PREDICTION FROM PARIS

Many years ago, my daughter worked at a charming, old-fashioned ice cream parlor and restaurant in New Hope called The Crystal Palace. It was the perfect job for a young teenager. She loved the Victorian atmosphere and the interesting mix of customers—a sprinkling of celebrities, a ton of tourists, and a steady stream of locals. Most of all, she loved her two bosses, Joe Meo and Joe Wiley.

The "Two Joes," as they were known throughout town, decided to leave Manhattan in the early '60s and settle down in New Hope. They ended up buying Odette Myrtil's house on Old Covered Bridge Road. (Odette, a Parisian actress who became famous for her starring roles on Broadway, owned a very popular restaurant on South River Road which she named after herself, Chez Odette.) The two Joes transformed the house into their own trendy and eclectic abode.

Hardworking and overflowing with creativity and talent, these two entrepreneurs took the town by storm in no time at all. Their New York panache, combined with their innate business skills led them to start one successful enterprise after another.

In addition to the restaurant, Joe Wiley also ran a gift shop at the corner of Bridge and Main called The Now and Then General Store where one could buy everything under the sun—from a bag of penny candy to a string of silk onions! As years went by, he eventually relocated the store to North Main Street and renamed it The Kaleidoscope. Occasionally, I would pop into Joe's store just to chit chat and exchange some town gossip. Of course, Joe was well aware of my interest in the supernatural and my reputation as a ghost hunter, but I always sensed that he was more of a skeptic than a believer.

"Let me know if anything unusual ever happens in your shop, Joe. It seems to me that a playful poltergeist could have a ball in here with all of the knick-knacks and bric-a-brac you have piled up from floor to ceiling." Joe would just look at me, raise his eyebrows, and quickly dismiss such a suggestion with a wave of his hand. "We'll see, Adi." He would then continue bustling around the shop, always busy and on the move until it was time to ring up the next customer's purchase on his huge, antique cash register.

One afternoon in the late autumn of 1983, I stepped into Joe's shop to say a quick hello since I had a little time to kill before conducting my next ghost tour.

"Have I got a story for you, Adi," Joe said as I walked through the door.

I was all ears as Joe proceeded to tell me about his most recent trip to Europe.

While in Paris, Joe was invited to attend a gala affair with some friends. It was a swanky, private party. The place was packed with an intriguing mixture of international guests. A real collection of "scene makers," as they would say. Joe mingled with the crowd and enjoyed making small talk with one person after another. But the piece de resistance of the evening was getting to meet the woman who at one time had served as a private advisor to the Shah of Iran. She was known to be one of the greatest psychics in all of Europe. Towards the end of the evening Joe was introduced to her.

The minute they met, she stared into Joe's eyes, and then, taking his hand in a firm grip between hers, she asked, "Where are you from?" "Oh," answered Joe, "from a very small place in Pennsylvania you've never heard of—New Hope." The psychic blinked her eyes a moment then nodded. "Tomorrow you will see this town mentioned on the first page of our Paris newspaper." Joe smiled and shook his head from side to side… "Oh, I can't believe that would ever happen. In such a small village, what could possibly occur that would be of interest in Paris?"

But, much to Wiley's amazement, headlines in the Paris newspapers on Monday, October 24, 1983, confirmed the psychic's strange prediction. "La Catastrophe Choque un Petit Village Americain." (A Catastrophe Shocks A Small American Village.) The article went on to report that "Jessica Savitch of NBC-TV was killed Sunday night, October 23, after the car she and her companion were in overturned and plunged into the Delaware Canal. The freak accident occurred in New Hope, Pennsylvania, a small rural town located in the southeastern part of the state."

Wow.

Joe Wiley was speechless.

Having experienced first hand the mysterious power of the "third eye" (the psychic ability to peer into the future), he returned home to the "petit village" of New Hope a skeptic no more.

A prediction from Paris finally convinced him that the supernatural world cannot be dismissed with just a wave of the hand.

C'est la vie.

*

*In reading my mother's account of this extraordinary experience of precognition, I wondered if the psychic was able to pick up any connection between the site where the accident occurred (adjacent to the parking lot of Chez Odette's restaurant) and the fact that Joe Wiley resided in the house which was once Odette Myrtil's former home. It is an interesting question to ponder.*

## THE FORTUNE TELLER OF FERRY STREET

Peering into the windows of The Jewel Tree was a feast for the eyes—brilliant gems and birthstones, shimmering gold and silver necklaces, gleaming pendants, pearls, rings and earrings, scores of bangles and bracelets, along with a fascinating array of crystals and amulets. How could any passerby resist such sparkling temptations? Furthermore, the sign outside the shop promised "Hundreds of One-of-a-Kind Pieces." Presiding over this mineral kingdom was Marie Bordner, a petite, blue-eyed woman who had the ability to not only assist you with your jewelry purchase but to also offer you a little of her psychic insight as well.

*Marie Bordner was a gemologist, a poet, and a gifted psychic.*

"I believe you must be looking for a topaz... am I right?

"May I suggest a tourmaline? It would increase your artistic talents.

"You need the energy of a transparent Yang stone. Be sure to wear it on your index or ring finger."

Before opening her jewelry boutique on Ferry Street, Marie Bordner had spent over twenty years in the world of advertising. "You see, I'm a Virgo," she'd say. "I was born under the sun sign of Mercury. Those born under this sign have the special gift to analyze and clarify ideas and then communicate them to others. I've always been interested in working with words." For many years, Marie lived the fast-paced life of a successful business woman. She wrote commercials for leading radio stations and then went on to write ads for national magazines such as *Seventeen* and *Vogue*. It was a hectic job. She was managing as many as twelve different advertising accounts at one time. And, then one day, she decided to get off the merry-go-round. She retired from advertising, moved away from the Germantown area of Philadelphia, and settled down in New Hope to follow her bliss.

"There's something very special about this little village," she said. "I believe it's encircled by an aura of strong, positive energy—it's a creative, playful, and inspiring energy. I can't think of a better place for a 'new beginning' than New Hope."

Enjoying more leisure time than ever before, Marie decided to pursue the three things that had always been closest to her heart: the world of poetry, the world of gems, and the supernatural world.

Needless to say, the two of us had very similar interests and it didn't take long for our paths to cross.

I shall never forget my first encounter with Marie. It was on a cold, blustery December day many years ago. I had just finished putting in a full day's work at my writing studio in Lambertville. As was my usual custom, I stopped at the Logan Inn for a piece of pie and a cup of hot tea before heading home. After finishing up my late afternoon snack, I left the inn and began walking quickly to my parked car. It was starting to get dark and I didn't want to worry my husband by arriving home too late. After taking just a few steps, however, I suddenly turned my head and looked across the street. A gorgeous, glimmering display case of jewels caught my eye! "Ahhh," I thought to myself, "I'm going to make a quick dash in there and see if I can find one more special Christmas gift for Lynda." No luck. The shop had closed at 5:00 p.m. and I was obviously just a little too late. Never one to give up easily, however, I peered through the door and noticed a diminutive, gray-haired lady bustling about in the shop. She heard my tapping and immediately walked over to unlock the door. "Hello there. May I help you?" she asked in a gracious and friendly tone. Although it was after hours, Marie welcomed me in. "Take your time and look around. I live upstairs above the shop so I can stay here as long as you like. There's no need for me to hurry home."

As I was browsing around, the first thing that caught my eye was a very unusual, silver, gem-encrusted brooch in the shape of a bow. A vintage piece for sure. I passed over it quickly. After all, this was not a time for me to be buying a piece of jewelry for myself. I needed a gift for my daughter. I continued to admire and examine one jeweled treasure after another, however, nothing seemed to ring a bell.

It was then that Marie drew my attention to two particular items. She had placed a cameo necklace and a silver bracelet on a velvet display mat for my closer inspection. At first glance, I dismissed both pieces. "The cameo looks too matronly for my daughter and the silver bracelet is much too plain. Probably a gold charm for her bracelet would be the best bet." Marie did not respond to my charm suggestion, she simply picked up the cameo necklace and asked me to look closely at the carving. It was the face of William Shakespeare.

In a split second, my eyes started to tear up. I gently rubbed my fingers over the carving of The Bard and thought of my dear father. At one time in his life, he had been a Shakespearian actor. How I missed him so much. Particularly at this time of year. She then handed me the slim, silver cuff bracelet. As I slipped it on my wrist, I had no doubt about the significance of this piece. For as long as I could remember, my mother wore a bracelet on her right wrist that was a near duplicate of this one. More tears trickled down my face. How did this woman, a complete stranger, know that these two objects in her store would evoke such deep and poignant memories for me?

Caught up unexpectedly in a wave of grief, there were no words for me to speak. Marie broke the silence as she grasped both of my hands in hers and said to me, "It's okay, dear. Love never dies."

"How does she know?" I thought to myself.

I quickly dried my eyes, thanked Marie for her hospitality and assistance, and walked out of the shop that evening, not buying a thing but cognizant of the fact that something quite remarkable and unexplainable had just happened.

I knew I would be back.

After the holidays were over, I stopped by to see Marie once again and asked her if she would like to join me for a cup of tea. "I'd love to," she said, "and I'd love to read your tea leaves, Adi." I wasn't surprised to learn that Marie had been doing tea leaf divination for many, many years. After our brief encounter in the jewelry store, it was clear to me that she was very clairvoyant.

Over tea, the two of us chatted for hours and hours. I told her about my interest in the paranormal. She told me about some of her earliest psychic experiences. From the time she was in her early teens, Marie realized she had telepathic powers. "I would hear a voice clearly telling me something," she said, "or perhaps, I would see a vision. I would see something as if I was having a dream, but I knew I was awake. Clairvoyance is like a memory that flashes across your mind's eye but you know it's not a memory.

"Minor psychic experiences happen to me all the time. Small things I've grown accustomed to. For example, I'll know exactly what someone is going to say before the words come out of their mouth. Often I'll know who's calling me before I pick up the phone. Time after time, I have customers coming into my shop looking for a birthstone ring and without asking which stone, I hand them 'their month.'"

"I believe you," I said.

"And now I have one more question. Can you tell me what made you pull out that Shakespeare cameo necklace and that silver cuff bracelet when I walked into your shop for the first time a few weeks ago?"

Marie just shrugged her shoulders. "You know, Adi, I always say to my customers... 'You do not choose your gemstone, but rather it chooses you.' I believe in the unerring truthfulness of that statement. Every stone and every piece of jewelry in my shop has its own magical power. There is a certain force field around minerals and metals that is not visible nor felt by the majority of people, but it's there. Jewelry is not just an article of adornment. Each piece contains a sustainable source of energy. Stones are precious. They can protect you, guide you, serve you and heal you. Based on the mineral content, every gemstone can affect the body, mind, spirit and heart. I believe people are naturally drawn to what they need. The wisdom and knowledge of the stone's energy speaks to the person's subconscious. Without knowing it, the stone chooses them.

"So it's a simple as that, Adi. I think the Shakespeare cameo necklace and the silver cuff bracelet both *chose you*."

I listened intently and nodded my head in agreement. From the moment I first stepped into The Jewel Tree I had felt an instant rapport with Marie.

"Now I would like to tell you a story," I said. "This is not only a very personal story it is also a deeply tragic one. But I want to tell it to you, because I know you will understand.

"Over twenty years ago, my mother and father were involved in a terrible car accident as they left our house to drive back to New York City on Christmas night. Neither one of my parents survived. It was such a tremendous shock to me and such an insufferable loss, that I thought I would never recover. I couldn't imagine ever being able to celebrate Christmas again. All these years since that fateful night, I have saved two small items that were taken from the scene of the accident. The slim, silver cuff bracelet which was removed from my mother's wrist by the ambulance driver and the well-worn, soft calfskin, double compartment coin purse which bore my father's monogrammed initials. Inside one compartment, I found a few coins. Inside the other compartment, there was a folded slip of paper with a quote which my father had copied down in his own handwriting. It said 'Love all, trust few, do wrong to none. ~ Shakespeare.'"

*Treasured items: a silver cuff bracelet that once belonged to the author's mother and a vintage Hobe pin that was a gift from AKTJ's dearest friend.*

I told Marie that I thought she must have had some intuitive knowledge of that deep sadness that was still buried within my heart. Her clairvoyant "knowing" led her to pick out those two particular pieces of jewelry for me as I walked into her shop on that cold, December evening just a few days before Christmas. It was clear from the moment we met, Marie Bordner understood the contents of my heart.

The two of us reached across the table to grasp hands once again.

Marie has read my tea leaves many times over the years. She has taken out her tarot cards from their red silk wrapper and done a reading for me on several occasions. She has told my fortune using her bag of seven crystal beads. I know enough to pay attention to the reoccurrence of certain symbols and the visions that she "sees." Even if Marie's predictions have sounded a bit crazy at the time, future events have usually born out the truth of her words.

Marie and I have also enjoyed sharing poetry together. "I believe the poet's job is to make people more aware of the virtues of people and the beauties of the world and other things. If one of my poems inspires someone to become more aware, or to reach a higher consciousness, then I will feel I have made my contribution to the world."

There is no question that Marie has used her talents and psychic gifts to bring help, healing, awareness and enlightenment to others. Her "one-of-a-kind" jewels have also brought much happiness (and "positive energy," as Marie would say) to many people.

Each time that I fasten on my silver bow-knot pin (a surprise gift to me from my dear friend, Rochelle), I can still hear Marie saying, "Of course, this brooch chose you, Adi. You know the underlying meaning of a bow motif don't you? It symbolizes 'The Tie That Binds.'"

It was my good fortune to meet Marie Bordner many years ago. Our friendship has been woven together by the ties that bind us— not only to each other, but to the Unknown World as well.


## BUCKS COUNTY'S BONA FIDE WITCH

Did you know that at one time Bucks County was home to a very glamorous, self-proclaimed witch? Her real name was Mrs. Mary Manners Hammerstein but everyone called her Hexie. Charming in manner, titian-haired and creamy-complexioned, she certainly did not look the part of a witch Yet, take a black night wanly lit by a watery moon and place Mrs. Hammerstein on her hilltop, gowned in her black hooded witch's cape, and she would be most believable. To Hexie Hammerstein and her witch conclave at Sky Island, psychic phenomena was a not only a philosophy, it was a way of life.

And what you may ask was Sky Island?

If you followed a long, winding road leading out from the village of Upper Black Eddy, you would eventually arrive at this unique place. "It's a hundred acres of beautiful, wooded land, but it's so much more than that," said Hexie. "It's a sacred space that stretches as high as you can think."

*Hexie Hammerstein*

Mrs. Hammerstein (the widow of Oscar Hammerstein's younger brother, Reginald), found this vast piece of property quite by accident. "To be honest with you, it didn't look like much at the time. Basically, it was nothing but a tiny, non-descript, shingled farm house surrounded by acres and acres of undeveloped land. But, I didn't see that. In my mind's eye, I saw a glorious setting for all kinds of things—a tall tower, a house with diamond shaped window panes, flowering plants, a glistening fish pond, an elaborate herb garden, an ice skating rink, a tennis court. And I whispered to myself, 'All of these things shall come to pass.'

"I didn't hesitate a second," the effusive Mrs. H. told me. "I bought the property, made sketches for the new house I envisioned, and hired a contractor who understood the whole concept of Sky Island. I wanted this to be a 'magical elsewhere,' a world set apart, a sanctuary of natural beauty, a dwelling place of peace and contentment."

Hexie, along with her coven of five witches, pitched in and assisted with the work load. "We blended our energies," she said. "Everything came together perfectly. It was all meant to be."

The expansive, sixteen room farm house was set high on a hilltop. A fifty foot tower covered with hand-split shingles gave it an eerie, medieval look. It wasn't long before Sky Island became a gathering place for anyone interested in living a "magickal life." Hexie cordially welcomed witches from far and near, parapsychologists and their followers, and any person who was committed to making a better life for themselves.

The first entrance into Sky Island was through the "Great Door" of the tower designed by Ernest E. Schaible, a Bucks County builder and furniture maker. From there, one followed a passageway that connected to the grand room. Stepping into the living quarters, my eyes were immediately drawn to the dramatic black hooded cloak hanging on a hook. "It's two hundred years old," Hexie explained to me. "At one time it belonged to a Scots woman who was a member of a witch's clan herself. It was given to me as a gift. I don't place much value on material things, but I must admit, this cloak is very dear to me."

"Does every witch have a cape?" I asked. I was curious to learn more about the significance of this particular garment.

"Most likely they do. A flowing cape allows nature's magnetic energy to move freely around the body. And, besides, witches spend a lot of time outdoors communing with Mother Earth so a cape is practical, it keeps us warm. It's as simple as that."

"And why black?" I asked. (Mrs. H. was such a colorful personality that I imagined she would be just the one to break the mold by donning a bright red cape!) "Oh, I don't need anymore color than what I have naturally," she said. A playful smile crossed her face as she tossed her head back and let her waist-long locks of silky, red hair fly through the air.

"Besides, I love black! It's such a mysterious and powerful color, you know. Unfortunately, it's often associated with darkness and evil, but think about it, what color do priests and nuns wear? Black is protective and absorbing. It's like a solar battery, it draws energy and light into one's whole being."

As we sat down together in front of a warm, crackling fire, Hexie served me one of her house specialties, Quiche Lorraine, seasoned with all kinds of fresh herbs and spices. "When I cook, I like to throw everything in!" she laughed.

The two of us talked for hours. I was absolutely fascinated by this woman's zest for life, her "fairy-tale" love story, and the unusual spiritual path she has chosen.

"So, tell me, Hexie, how did you end up being Oscar Hammerstein's sister-in-law?"

"Oh, for as long as I can remember, I've loved the theater," she said. "And, it was this passion that ultimately brought Reggie and me together.

"In 1943, I was living outside of Chicago and I had a friend, Harry Stockwell, who was playing the male lead in Oklahoma. I was dying to play the role of Ado Annie, so I went to Harry and asked him how I could break into the show. He told me to wait until Hammerstein arrived and then I could do my audition for him. (Reginald Hammerstein was the general stage director for the *Oklahoma* companies.) Of course, I knew there was an Oscar Hammerstein, but I didn't know he had a brother who was also in the theater business, too. So this was all news to me.

"One night I ended up going to see the show with a girlfriend. The two of us sat down and started flipping through the program. The theater was buzzing with anticipation and all of a sudden I felt a tingly sensation rolling over me. I looked up and noticed a tall man standing in the wings across the stage. I had no idea who he was but I felt drawn to him immediately. At the time I was divorced and I had absolutely no intention of ever getting married again, but I took one look at this stranger and I nudged my girlfriend and said 'See that tall man over there? I'm going to marry him!' Of course, Rae thought I was nuts. She just shook her head and said, 'Mary, you're crazy! You don't even know him!'

"Something else extraordinary happened that same night.

Standing next to this strange man (who, by the way, turned out to be Reginald Hammerstein), I noticed a little blonde girl. The child never appeared in the show, so I was curious to know who she was. Later on in the evening, I asked Reginald about her. He looked completely puzzled and said, 'What on earth are you talking about? There was no little girl standing next to me.'

"Now, I know that the child I saw that night was the daughter we were to have. Reggie (named after her father) is a tow-headed blonde and the spitting image of her dad. You see, Adi, I *know* from experience that there are other senses and other dimensions."

Needless to say, Hexie never auditioned for the part. The stranger she spotted that evening across the crowded room proposed to her that very same night.

Unfortunately, their "happily ever after" ending was cut short about ten years later.

One afternoon when Mrs. Hammerstein was helping her daughter get dressed for a party, she heard a loud blast. "It was a shattering noise. I was absolutely shaken to the core." Shortly thereafter, she learned that the explosion occurred at the precise moment her husband (who was miles away from home) had suffered a heart attack and died.

"Soon after he 'crossed over,' something strange happened. I was tidying up Reggie's playroom and I distinctly felt the presence of someone standing behind me. I was terrified. I turned around and there was RKH. I saw his shoes and the trousers of his dark blue suit. For a moment, I was immobilized. You know, you're always afraid of the unknown—no matter what!

"For years afterwards, I was aware of his presence in the house. I would feel him sitting on the edge of my bed at night. Sometimes, he'd pull the covers over me. Or he would stand behind me while I was in the bathroom washing my face or braiding my hair. I grew very used to his presence. In a way, it was comforting to me to know he was still here—still looking after me. I liked that."

After her husband's death, Mrs. Hammerstein purchased Sky Island and formed a coven of witches. The group used to meet from time to time at her Sky Island house to discuss psychic phenomena, parapsychology and extra-sensory perception. Each witch member had her own broom which was stored at Sky Island. The members also had identifying names such as Brighid (exalted one), Athena (wise one), Meaveen (intoxicating), Thalia (flourishing), and Selena (moon goddess). Of course, Mrs. Hammerstein was always known as Hexie (little witch or nice witch), the nickname she was dubbed with as a child.

I asked Mrs. Hammerstein point blank… "What is witchcraft?"

"Oh my! Witchcraft is the oldest religion in the world. It's been around for thousands of years. It actually predates the majority of well-known religions. In ancient times, it was referred to as the 'craft of the wise.' The people who headed up the various religions in those days, the high priests and priestesses, were said to be 'magic makers.' They were thought to have powers that no one else had—a supernatural ability to control and influence things. What they really had, I believe, was the power of *thought*. That's the problem today. Most people don't use their minds. They don't think.

"I tell those who come here that they can have anything they want. Thoughts are powerful and whatever one thinks about will come to be. Whether we know it or not, we all have a 'sixth sense.' Everyone is born with ESP capability, it's a primordial sense. We all possess it, but not everybody develops it or uses it. What a waste! Those of us who are visionaries, who can see with the 'third eye,' we must be careful to use our extra-sensory powers wisely. The one rule we adhere to at Sky Island is 'Harm None.' We don't do anything that might hurt someone else or deprive them from having the good things they want."

Hexie continued to expound on her Wiccan beliefs. "To me the truth is to be that which you want. When you know what you want, you become a magnet. You draw to yourself everything you need. I think this is the biggest hang-up today, most people have no idea of what they *really* want.

"I believe that *feeling* is the whole secret of life. Feelings shape our destiny. And most people fear real feeling. But intense emotions hold tremendous power. This is what fills our memory bank! And, whether we realize it or not, it's our subconscious, or our memory bank, that controls ninety percent of our choices. So, the most important question to ask is 'What's in that bank? What feelings are you holding on to and how are they serving you?' You've got to dig down inside yourself and search for the truth.

"I don't want to go through just the motions of life. I want to feel and experience everything at the depths of my being. And, I want to entertain only those feelings which contribute to my own happiness and to the happiness of the world. Every day I strive to live in harmony with all that is seen and unseen."

It was clear to me that Mrs. Hammerstein was not only a dynamic personality, she was also a deep thinker.

Still curious to learn more, I asked her about some of the paranormal activities that I've investigated myself.

I asked Hexie to tell me about … hexes!

"Oh, I could place a hex on anyone if I wanted to. A hex is nothing more than hypnosis. But why would I do such a thing? I'd only be hurting myself. That's one of the basic rules in witchcraft, whatever you do to others (good or bad) comes back to you three fold. I believe in blessings, not curses. I want to take my energy and put it to good use."

"What about séances?" I asked.

"Well, what the heck is a séance? Today it's more of a form of entertainment than real spiritual communication. You get a bunch of people sitting around in the dark, joining hands and trying their best to contact a dead person. And, maybe they do and maybe they don't. Who's to say? But no, we don't do that here. Séances are valid to those who believe they are. But I can call in anybody, alive or so-called dead, that I want to. I just go to the mind. Where else can you go when you want to know something? Our subconscious mind holds all the answers. I truly believe that."

"Have you had any spiritualists visit you here at Sky Island?" I asked.

"Yep, I've had a lot of them here. You know, the ones who belong to a union and they come here full of themselves, waving their cards in the air. They go into trances. They contact the spirit world. They do whatever you want. It's how they make their living. Some are sincere. Some are charlatans. And, most of them, if you ask me, are on an ego trip. Personally, I think those people who are forever running to attend a séance or consult a spiritualist are so hooked on the hereafter that they can't handle the Now. I try to stay focused on the present moment. This is the only time there is. That's my belief and that's enough for me."

Unfortunately, the time had come for me to go. As I made my departure through the doorway of the Grand Tower, Hexie left me with these final words (from the *Witches Rede*):

"What you send forth comes back to thee,
So ever mind the Law of Three.
Follow this with mind and heart,
Merry ye meet, and merry ye part."

What a pleasurable and thought-provoking afternoon it had been. I left Sky Island with a sense of merriment swirling all around me.

*

*Hexie Hammerstein was a well-known personality in the Bucks County area for many years. In addition to being an active spokeswoman for Wiccan beliefs, she was also a gourmet cook who celebrated the benefits of vegetarian cuisine long before it became the current trend. In the 1960s, she occasionally hosted cooking shows which were televised live from her Sky Island kitchen. Using home-grown herbs and fresh produce, Hexie shared her knowledge and enthusiasm for healthy eating and living.*

# ONGOING EERIE ENCOUNTERS

Mystery hovers over all things here below.

*

*Alphonse Lamartine*

# SPIRITS FROM CHRISTMAS PAST

One year I hosted a special Ghost Tour event during the Christmas Season. The festivities took place at the old McKonkey Ferry Inn located in Washington Crossing at Washington Crossing State Park. The Ferry Inn was the place where Washington ate his Christmas dinner and finalized his plans prior to the famous crossing of the Delaware on the evening of December 25, 1776. What a night that was! As we all know, Washington's daring military move was a pivotal moment in our nation's history. The surprise attack and his victory in Trenton changed the whole course of the American Revolution.

*The McKonkey Ferry Inn (built in 1750) at Washington Crossing Park is said to be haunted by Revolutionary soldiers.*

I arrived at the Ferry Inn with my dear friend, Adele Gamble, who was also serving as one of my Ghost Tour guides at the time. As the evening got started, the two of us were intent on taking care of all the logistics for this festive gathering. We were busy getting people seated, lighting candles (there is no electricity in the inn), and setting up a place for the musician who would be performing.

After everyone was settled in, I welcomed our guests, gave a few introductory comments, and then introduced the young lady who would be entertaining us that night on her dulcimer. She started to play, gracefully sliding the backs of her fingers across the instrument. The little hammers struck out the tunes that Washington loved best. The music was charming and evocative. Adele and I were sitting with our backs to the doorway that led to the tavern room behind us.

In the middle of this delicate music we began to hear a loud scraping and scratching of furniture along the floor in the rear tavern room. It was as though people were pushing chairs around and moving tables. It was a loud rumble and very disturbing. I thought to myself, "Who could be so thoughtless as to make all of this noise in the middle of our concert?" One of the officers of the park was present that evening and walked over and looked through the doorway. Obviously, he was aware of the disruption, too. Adele and I turned around and peered over our shoulders. Immediately the noise stopped.

A few minutes later, my friend and I quickly exchanged glances again. We both heard the soft but distant sound of booted feet pacing the tavern floor. Then the pacing stopped and all was quiet.

After the concert was over and we had finished our refreshments, I asked the park officer what he thought caused the noise in the tavern room. He said, "Oh, it must have been the hostess who lives upstairs." I asked him if he could please give me her name. The next day I was able to track her down. She was quite incensed when I gently questioned her about the noise in the Tavern Room. "Heavens, I made a point of being very quiet. I purposely took off my shoes, sat down in a chair, and didn't move a muscle. I could hear the beautiful sounds of the zither being played. I enjoyed the concert as much as you did." Then she added, "But, I must admit—I heard all of that rumpus in the Tavern Room, too. I wondered what on earth was going on down there."

So it was not the hostess. Adele and I talked about the experience for long afterwards. We concluded that the timing of our festive celebration at the Ferry Inn was very close to one of the most dramatic events in history. We feel that Washington must have paced back and forth along that area just prior to the crossing. I believe the emotional energy of that deeply traumatic and anxious moment has remained fixed in a kind of mental atmosphere. On

There had once been an old man who used to check the empty place out from time to time but he'd been dead for over six months. John leaned to his right and stared closely. The light moved past each of the front windows of the stone structure; then as Kennedy watched closely, he saw the rickety farm house door slowly open. In the next minute a figure emerged. It started to come towards him. It was a man and he was carrying a lantern. As he came closer, Kennedy saw that the tall figure was dressed in a buff and blue uniform and on his head he wore a gold-braided tricorn.

John could hardly believe his eyes. Could it be some kind of watchman? But who would be guarding a house in ruins; who would be doing so with an old-fashioned lantern rather than a flashlight and why would he be dressed in a Revolutionary uniform? None of the questions could John answer to himself in the seconds that followed. He could only quickly come to terms with the comforting fact that he was not alone and that someone was coming to help him. He climbed out of his car and rushed towards the front of it just as the other man stepped into the roadway. His eyes were focused straight ahead and they glimmered in the lantern light.

"I say, sir, I do appreciate your coming in the frigid cold to help...," started John.

The figure passed in front of the car, the headlights highlighting every detail of his gold-braided uniform. The man scarcely blinked. His footsteps never slowed nor hurried. He kept walking steadily on, passing across the front of the car and right on past Kennedy as though nothing were there but the road itself.

"Sir," called Kennedy. "I wonder if you could..." The tall man kept on walking, his head turning neither to one side or the other. His eyes looked only straight ahead as though he were intent on reaching some goal on the other side of the road. John turned gradually, scarcely believing what he was seeing. The man gave not the slightest response to Kennedy in either word or glance. Indeed, he did not seem to be aware that there was anything present in that roadway but himself and his flickering lantern.

Kennedy pulled his coat collar tighter around his throat as he stared, transfixed at the uniformed figure. The straight form moved steadily across the stretch of ground until it reached the ruins of the old grist mill. In the next second, the figure, pale lantern light and all, vanished in the dark recesses of the ancient mill.

Kennedy swallowed hard. He was shaken. Had he seen an apparition? He couldn't believe that. There was nothing ghostly about the figure. It had been solid. Surely he had been flesh and blood. Hadn't his car's headlights showed every mortal detail?

Yet he began to recall those eyes. Somehow, they did not seem to belong to any living being of this world.

*The Thompson-Neely House is thought by some to be the place where Washington and others planned the surprise attack against the Hessian forces at Trenton.*

John shook a shiver off and climbed back into the car. He pressed his foot once more on the accelerator. The car started without flinching. In a very short time, he was home. As he warmed himself near the kitchen stove and his wife heated up some coffee for him, John told the strange story.

Yvonne believed her husband. So do I.

It is interesting to me that in 1944 there was no general knowledge that the Thompson-Neely house was an important historic building. No one except a few in-depth historians were aware that it was in that old farm house that Washington and his generals met in a strategy conclave to make the crucial decision to cross the frozen Delaware.

Did General Washington, or one of his generals, leave the meeting and cross the river path to an encampment by the grist mill? Did he ever carry a lantern to light his way?

Did John Kennedy, some century and a half later, a man who himself highly patriotic and sensitive to the cause for freedom, somehow, on that snow-still night, "tune-in" psychically to a traumatic event in our country's past history? Was he able to pick it up, so to speak, re-seeing it, much as one plays over again a recording or movie of some past event?

Personally, I believe that is was happened.

In any case, the setting for this remarkable ghost story is now open to the public. The Thompson-Neely house (which has been restored) is a National Historic Landmark. It is known today as the "House of Decision."


## HAUNTED WOODS AND BURIED GOLD

One of Bucks County's most famous landmarks, Bowman's Tower, is located along scenic River Road just south of New Hope. It is impossible to miss the imposing 100 ft. tower that sits perched on top of a wooded area known as Bowman's Hill.

Visitors flock here to see the spot where Washington's army camped out during the Revolutionary War. They come to enjoy the marvelous views of the Delaware River Valley which can be seen from the top of the sky-high stone tower. They come to visit the wildflower preserve, to hike the trails, to do some bird watching and, perhaps, some outdoor picnicking. And, from what I have learned, there are also those who come here with old maps and shovels to do some digging in search of pirate's gold!

Legend has it that centuries ago, Captain William Kidd, a dashing Scottish swashbuckler, was hired by the British government to rid the seas of pirates. The ship's surgeon was alleged to be an

*Bowman's Tower is located on a steep hillside that borders River Road.*

Englishman named Dr. John Bowman. After a time, however, the task took a twist. Kidd found the crime he was hired to stop far more thrilling and enriching than the police work in which he was engaged. He hoisted the black flag and turned pirate himself! It is reputed that Kidd and his crew were one of the cruelest bands of pirates that ever sailed the seas. The buccaneer's career was brief, however. In 1699, he was captured and sent to England for questioning by Parliament. He was eventually tried, and executed for piracy. After Kidd's death on the gallows, Dr. Bowman apparently escaped to America and hid out along the quiet banks of the Delaware River. Tradition says that he brought his share of the pirate loot with him—a chest full of gold estimated to be worth about $200,000. Where did he hide it? Aye, rumor has it that Dr. Bowman buried his cache of treasure somewhere on the hill. He loved the place so much that he also chose the hillside as his final resting place. "I want to be buried at the top o' the hill," he said. "It's as close to Heaven as I'll ever get!" And so he was buried in an unmarked grave at the top of the hill that bore his name from that time on.

For many years, the ground of Bowman's Hill was dotted with pits from those trying to find Bowman's share of the pirate loot captured under Captain Kidd. Well into the twentieth century, caves, creeks, and abandoned mine shafts were plumbed in concerted efforts to find the buried gold. One man showed up with a map that diagrammed the path to the buried treasure which he said had been passed down for generations in his family. Although many have dreamed of finding Dr. Bowman's hidden gold, I have never heard of anyone who was successful.

But I did meet someone who came close to it. He was a very interesting man named Brad Davis from Trenton, New Jersey. Brad told me the story that some thirty or forty years ago he had a friend named Fred Johnson, an old, retired railroad man who lived in Yardley, Pennsylvania. It seems that Fred had spent a lifetime thinking about the buried gold. He knew that at one time the London Company had opened a copper mine that penetrated the hill and included two considerable chambers and a central shaft. As it turned out, the copper ore was of a low grade and the business soon faded away. But, the shaft was still left and Fred was convinced that the gold was in that mine since nobody had been able to find it elsewhere. He figured it had probably slipped down to the bottom of the old shaft, which was reported to be about 250 ft. deep and was filled with water.

One day the two men decided to go exploring. Fred had complete knowledge of the hill and the surrounding topography. The men found the abandoned mine shaft and crawled in some 60 ft. to the edge of the water-filled cave. They let down grappling hooks attached to wires. At first they brought up only pieces of old wood pilings but in the process they discovered that the shaft had filled in until it was only about 30 ft. deep. They lowered the hooks again, and this time they brought up a box about 4 by 2 ft. wide and 2 ft. deep. The box was so heavy that they could hardly lift it. Fred reached down into the broken top and brought up a handful of water-soaked parchment so soggy it was illegible. At that moment, the lid broke off and the box fell back into the shaft.

Fred and Brad were both certain the buried treasure was in that box but they knew the shaft would have to be pumped out in order to reach it. They asked the members of the Trenton Fire Company to do it, but they refused, saying the job would cost too much and there was no guarantee they would find anything of value. More than that, the job was much too risky since there was a good chance the mine could cave in at any time.

So, Johnson and Davis finally gave up.

In doing research for this story, Brad was more than willing to take me to that old cave on the hillside. Today the opening is much too small for a human being to fit through. But to this day, or until the day he took me there (which was about 1980) he wholeheartedly believed there was some kind of treasure down there.

Be that as it may, the hillside all along the South River Road is full of rumors and legends of buried gold and ghostly pirates guarding it. Some say that John Bowman's restless spirit rises out of his unmarked grave on the hillside and haunts the wooded area. He appears and disappears, he shrieks and groans, but as far as I know, he has never revealed to anyone the spot where his gold was hidden.

Bowman's Hill is now state-owned property and it is illegal to dig for anything on the premises. Fortune seekers, be warned, you must look elsewhere if you decide to embark on a gold-hunting adventure.

I believe the hillside does offer riches, however, which are neither elusive nor illegal. The real riches of Bowman's Hill are found in its natural beauty. So leave your shovel at home and enjoy the naturally-created, breathtaking treasures that this beautiful vista offers throughout all seasons of the year.

# A VOICE IN THE NIGHT

Just outside of New Hope, one of Bucks County's most historic inns, the Centre Bridge Inn, sits perched on the Delaware River overlooking the canal. The inn, once known as the old Mitchell's Ferry Inn from 1796 to 1813 until the ferry was discontinued, became the possession of Arthur Fretz in 1909. His daughter, Virginia, was born and raised in the old inn.

It was an interesting life, living in a place that was the hub and center of activity for the village. Of all the many incidents which occurred, the following story is the one Virginia Fretz Evans of Doylestown loved best to tell me about.

*The Centre Bridge Inn. Ethereal sounds manifest themselves on this site.*

During the time that Arthur Fretz owned the inn near the bridge, a wealthy widow lived on a farm close to the tavern. One rainy night a knock came at the door to her house. She opened it and found a handsome young man standing there. His frayed coat was sodden wet. His hair streamed in dripping curls over his eyes. He spoke with a voice as musical as chimes.

"Pardon the likes of such a shabby visitor, but it's cold and weary I am, and I'd appreciate your allowin' me the courtesy of sleepin' in your barn." He looked sideways at the stone barn off to his left and back at the woman.

She hesitated.

"I'll be off in the mornin', I shall." He flashed a smile that looked to her like the blessing of an angel.

Suddenly, the widow opened the door wide. "Come on in, young man. You'll catch your death of pneumonia. If you haven't the sense to know that, I do." She pushed him towards the warm fire sputtering in the quiet room. "Here, take off your coat and shirt. I'll get a suit of my husband's. It will fit you well enough until your own clothes are dry."

She disappeared into the adjoining room. The young man removed his coat, smiling. He looked around about him at the shining pewter tea pot on a nearby table. The rugs looked of the finest thick wool. He rubbed his hands together over the fire and felt as pleased and comfortable as if he'd been in the house for weeks.

The widow insisted the young Irishman take the guest room for the night. She took him a cup of hot coffee. "You know," she said, "there's no reason for you to leave in the morning. Why don't you stay on a while? I could use a hand with the farm chores at this time of year."

The Irishman grinned. His eyes sparkled like blue gems over the oil lamp as he set it down on a table at the head of the guest bed. "Nothin' could appeal more to the likes of me. I thank ye heartily."

The young man stayed for weeks that pushed on into months. One day before the year was up, he married the widow.

From the day he had arrived, the whole village had been aware of the happy-go-lucky Irishman down at the widow's farm. At the inn, he was as familiar as the owner, Arthur Fretz, himself. Evening after evening, the young man sauntered across to the inn and had his mugs of ale and his lighthearted hours of pleasure singing the songs of his homeland.

One night, Fretz's little baby girl was crying. Her wails floated into the tavern bar until the Irishman could stand it no longer.

"I say, let me have the little one for a moment. All she needs is a lullaby to soothe her wee unhappy heart." In moments, the young man had the baby lifted out of the cradle and into his arms. He moved over next to the fireplace and sat down, swinging her gently to and fro in his arms.

Then the lullaby began. His light voice rose pure and clear through the smoke-filled air. The rough-hewn river boatmen put down their mugs and listened. They heard him every night, but this time the song was the most enchanting. In no time at all, the baby did fall asleep.

Virginia recounted this tale of the bewitching Irishman who lulled her to rest that night with the same delight that her father had told the story so many times.

For the widow, the tale was not a happy one to recollect. Not too long after their marriage, the young man gathered what money and possessions he could and departed. Neither the widow or anyone in the village ever heard from him again.

Yet he was never quite forgotten. Nor could the widow be completely unforgiving. For a time, the young Irishman with the eyes and smile and voice of angels had brought a sparkle and gaiety to a quiet river town.

As an interesting follow-up to this story, recently I was talking with the owner of the Centre Bridge Inn, Stephen DuGan, and he corroborated a strange incident that I had heard myself when I was talking to Ann Miller several years ago. Ann, a noted stage singer and dancer, used to love to come to Bucks County. She had spent several weekends at the inn. On one occasion when Stephen was talking to her, the two of them became aware of a presence in the hallway. They both realized somebody or something was there. There seemed to be a kind of misty form of a person at the foot of the stairs. They spoke to the presence but there was no answer and I am wondering... was that an Irish tenor coming back looking for a cradle?

*

*The Centre Bridge Inn, a 200 year old historic property, overlooks the Delaware River in the quaint, little village of Centre Bridge. The inn, located just two miles north of New Hope, offers impressive dining and lodging. It is well known as a "Special Occasions" destination.*

# Room of the Ghostly Bells

The Lambertville House has always been one of my most favorite old inns. Its history dates back to the early 1800s when an enterprising young congressman named John Lambert saw the potential and need for a hostelry to accommodate the enormous number of travelers moving along the stage coach route between New York and Philadelphia. He built an inn which he called at first simply "The Stage House." The inn became famous for its impressive design, its fancy iron grill work, and its unusually large capacity. The three-story structure boasted fifteen guest rooms along with a long, low-ceilinged dining room, and two comfortable parlors heated by open fireplaces. The popular hostelry also advertised a bridal suite that offered "the utmost in comfort and luxury."

From the earliest times, this charming inn became a busy stopping point for a multitude of discerning travelers. The old registry, which used to be kept on display in the room called "The Buttery," listed a host of fascinating guests including General Ulysses S. Grant, President Andrew Jackson, and "General Tom Thumb," the dwarf who achieved international fame performing with P.T. Barnum. In fact, legend has it that Tom Thumb (his real name was Charles Stratton) and his wife, Lavinia (who matched her husband in size and height), occupied the Bridal Suite sometime following their elaborate wedding ceremony in New York and the private reception which Abraham Lincoln hosted for the famous little couple at the White House.

As one century turned into another, the inn changed owners and went through many transformations. A front porch was added and additional rooms were annexed to the building, but the distinctive balustrades, columns and lattices shaped of a grape-leaf design remained the same.

In the late 1940s, the inn was bought by the Allen family. Mr. and Mrs. Allen were dedicated and appreciative proprietors of this historic property. They lived on the second floor of the inn. Everything was kept in meticulous order. The old, wide plank floors gleamed with care and polish. Every room was appointed with antique furnishings appropriate to the inn's historic background. Not only did Mrs. Allen assemble antique furniture and objects d'art, but most particularly, she had a fascination for bells. One of her greatest passions was collecting all different kinds of bells—silver, brass, copper, glass, porcelain, school bells, cow bells, Indian elephant bells, sleigh bells, dinner bells, whatever. She even had a tiny pair of crystal wedding bells which she loved to ring as a tribute to Tom Thumb and his wife.

Mrs. Allen kept her collection of bells in their private parlor, the same area which once constituted the original Bridal Suite of the old inn. One day, I had a chance to see this amazing collection for myself. The bells were assembled everywhere throughout the parlor. Some stood on book shelves, others were lined up on the fireplace mantel, or rested on the window sills. Some hung from a corner hook. As far as the eye could see, bells permeated the décor of this entire room.

After the Allens passed on, the inn came into the ownership of their son, Jack, who eventually moved away, taking the contents of the old Allen parlor with him.

Not too long after that, one of the hostesses named Marie who was working at the inn at the time had an experience that she has never forgotten. She was on duty in the main hall late one night when out of the dark stairway came the sound of a bell ringing. She followed the insistent tinkling up the steps to the second floor. Sure enough, it came from behind the closed door of the old Allen living room. She opened the door and entered the barren room in complete astonishment. A tiny gleam of moonlight penetrated through the windows casting shadows on the dark walls and the wide-planked floor, but even in the semi-darkness, she could see that the room was absolutely empty! It was nothing but a desolate and abandoned space. Marie turned on her heel and descended the staircase still shaking her head in disbelief.

Since the Allen's parlor was once the Bridal Suite of the old inn, I feel it must have housed in its psychic environment a lot of warmth and romance as well as the energy of its most recent occupant, Mrs. Allen.

Was there someone dining at the inn that night who unconsciously felt a rapport with Mrs. Allen's passion for bells? Or, perhaps, there were lovers staying at the inn for the evening who unknowingly tuned in to the amorous energy stored in the old Bridal Suite.

Marie will tell you. Someone, or something, caused one of those bells to start ringing again.

*

*The Lambertville House, located at 32 Bridge Street in Lambertville, New Jersey, is listed on the National Register of Historic Places. Under new ownership, the inn has gone through an extensive renovation and expansion. It reopened in 1997 as a luxurious, boutique hotel. The original Bridal Suite no longer exists, but lovers and newlyweds can enjoy a romantic stay in one of the hotel's spacious two-room Courtyard Suites.*

## "INN-VISIBLE" GUESTS

For years, Bucks County has been considered the perfect get-away destination for travelers both near and far. The New Hope area, in particular, is filled with a wide variety of charming and romantic inns. Visitors can choose from hotels, historic inns, and B&Bs nestled right in the heart of town or they can follow the winding River Road out of New Hope and pick from a medley of inns that dot the Delaware.

Apparently, the ghosts aren't choosey. They like to hang out everywhere in this area. They have been known to haunt the in-town spots as well as the rustic riverside lodges and inns.

The Wedgwood Inn, owned and operated by two of my favorite people, Carl and Nadine Glassman, is a New Hope treasure. The old, Victorian blue-colored "Painted Lady" sits on two acres of beautiful grounds. Inside the house, guests love to admire the collection of Wedgwood china that the Glassmans have collected throughout the years. Outside, guests can wander along the flower-lined brick walkways to view the award-winning gardens or, perhaps, head towards the old-fashioned gazebo located on the property.

*The apparition of American folk artist Joseph Pickett, has been seen in the gazebo located behind the historic New Hope Wedgwood Inn.*

Not too long ago, Carl told me that one of his patrons had a most unusual experience as she stepped outside and walked into the garden area. Crossing the lawn, she happened to catch sight of an artist who was standing in the Victorian gazebo. He had his easel set up and he was painting away. She was curious as to what he was painting so she strolled over to the gazebo to see if he would allow her to take a look at his canvas. As she got close to the gazebo, he suddenly faded away. The artist was gone and so was the easel. The gazebo was completely empty.

This story is interesting because Joseph Pickett, who earned posthumous fame as a primitive artist, was once New Hope's local town butcher and grocer. In the late 1800s, he operated a store on Mechanic Street. Occasionally, he would leave his butcher block to pursue a leisurely activity that he enjoyed—painting. It was a familiar sight to see him setting up his easel on a town corner, or a footpath, or along the hollowed valley below the Wedgwood Inn. (One can still see ruins of the old flax mills that were originally built in this small valley along the mouth of Ingham Creek. Most of the workers who were hired to toil in the mills had come over from Manchester, England. Therefore, Pickett, decided to name this small expanse of land "Manchester Valley.") His most famous painting, entitled *Manchester Valley*, which commemorates the coming of the railroad to New Hope, now hangs in the New York City Museum of Modern Art.

Joseph was a self-taught artist who loved painting scenes of the local landscape and the history of the area. Unfortunately, at the turn of the nineteenth century, no one had yet realized his greatness. After, his death, his wife, Emily, could hardly give his work away. Today, of course, he is recognized as one of America's greatest folk artists.

Maybe lack of appreciation in his own time explains why Joseph Pickett comes back so often to haunt the environs of the little town where he was born and where he died.

Over the years, a number of other guests at the Wedgwood have also spotted the phantom artist in the gazebo. Another interesting sighting was reported by a woman who strolled around the property and peeked into the gazebo to admire the painting an artist was working on. After her walk, she returned to the main house, only to find the very same picture hanging on the wall. (When they first opened the inn, the Glassmans decided to adorn one of the walls with a reproduction of Pickett's famous *Manchester Valley* painting.) She was completely baffled. "How on earth did you frame the painting so quickly?" she asked Carl.

His face broke into a smile. "Aha! Joseph must be out in the gazebo doing his thing again." He explained to his guest that it was not a painting but a print of the painting. He then gave her the scoop on the Pickett apparition which has been seen on and off at that very location for many, many years.

"I think we plopped that gazebo on the spot where Pickett liked to paint the most," said Carl. "So, what does he do? He just comes back, sets up his easel and resumes painting the scene he loved best—Manchester Valley."

The Wedgwood is also home to the ghost of a young slave girl who goes by the name of Sarah. "We thought we knew all the mysteries of the house after living here for so many years," said Carl, "but the Wedgwood is always full of surprises!" In the 1990s, Carl and Nadine made a couple of remarkable discoveries. First, they found a hidden staircase above the kitchen. Not long after, they discovered a hatch at the base of the gazebo in the back yard. But it wasn't until some years later when extensive renovations took place on the property, that the Glassmans were able to link these two discoveries together. As the front-loader was plowing through the inn's foundations, contractors discovered a 30 ft. long, 9 ft. high stone and wooden tunnel. The newly discovered tunnel connected the indoor secret staircase to the hatch outside. "I believe the tunnel was once a link to the Underground Railroad," mused Carl. "It fits in with the reported sightings of a young, fugitive ghost."

"We would hear the sounds of feet shuffling, along with a persistent tapping noise, coming from the wall next to the secret staircase," said Carl. Not long after, a psychic identified the restless spirit of a run-away Negro slave who got separated from her family. The ghost was given the name "Sarah." Her spirit exits today as a young girl in despair. Perhaps, "Sarah" was hidden in the secret staircase and separated from her parents who were in the tunnel.

Apparently, there is a telepathic linkage between "Sarah" and other young girls her age who have stayed at the inn. Over the years, the ghost of Sarah has appeared to at least three different 12-year-old girls. Sarah allegedly recounted to each one of them her gripping story of slavery, escape, hiding and separation. The young witnesses, staying at the Wedgwood years apart from each other, and with no previous knowledge of the inn's past history, each gave an identical account describing Sarah's appearance, her clothes, and her tragic situation. It would seem that centuries later the lost soul of a young slave girl is still seeking help from the living on her never-ending journey to freedom.

Leaving New Hope and crossing over the bridge to Lambertville, New Jersey, one can expect to find a warm welcome at another historic inn, The Lambertville House. Not surprisingly, this old hostelry, which opened in 1809, is filled with an eerie presence.

Just ask Chi Chi, who at one time worked as a hostess at the inn when Jack Allen was owner and proprietor of the establishment. Jack had acquired a priceless piece of artwork from his father. It was an original painting done by one of the most famous Pennsylvania impressionists, Edward W. Redfield. From time to time, Allen would put his treasured painting on display in the dining room for his patrons to enjoy. He had it proudly hanging on a back wall secured by a cordoned off area.

*The Lambertville House, located in Lambertville, New Jersey, has been welcoming guests since 1812 and is listed on the National Registry of Historic Places.*

At nighttime, it was the job of the hostess to remove the painting from the wall and return it to Allen's private office on the second floor. Chi Chi took this special duty to heart. On the first night she carried it up, however, she had the strangest feeling of being watched as she removed it from the dining room and carried it upstairs through the shadowy hallway. Following her boss's instructions, she took the painting to the office (which had once been the parlor room when Jack's parents lived over the hotel) and carefully placed it against the wall between the two windows in the room. "I kept looking over my shoulder, Adi. I had the strangest feeling that, somehow, someone had gotten into that old parlor and was staring at me and the painting."

The only light in the room was a faint glow from a small lamp. Chi Chi looked around in the semi-darkness... there was no one there. Uneasily, she left the room and locked the door behind her as she'd been instructed. She quickly finished up her hostess duties downstairs, gathered up her car keys and purse, and got ready to leave. Just as she was headed towards the front door, however, she heard a bell ringing from the old parlor. (As you'll recall, this paranormal activity of "ringing bells" was described in the previous story.) Chi Chi turned and ran back upstairs, unlocked the door, and peered in. As before, the room was empty.

Then, she nearly fainted when she made a startling discovery. In the dim light from the hall she could see that the Redfield painting was no longer facing out. Someone, or something, had turned it around. All she could see was the hanging wire secured to the back of the painting. She was flabbergasted.

Chi Chi has never gotten over that incident. To this day, she still wonders who it was, or what it was, that performed an "about-face" on Jack Allen's beloved painting.

About six miles north of New Hope, there is another historic inn which is located along the upper Delaware River in a tiny village called Lumberville. The Black Bass Inn (aptly named for the excellent fish found in the Delaware waters), is hauntingly beautiful in every sense of the word. Built in 1745, the original owners of this tavern and inn were ardent supporters of George III. Unfortunately, the American revolutionists would find no food or shelter at this particular inn. And one thing's for sure, George Washington did not sleep here!

Herbert Ward purchased the property in 1945 and created a most inviting restaurant and lodging facility. In nice weather, guests could enjoy dining on the long, screened-in veranda that overlooked the canal. There was also the cozy dining room that featured a large, open fireplace. The medieval décor in this room was punctuated by an array of pierced tin lanterns hanging from the ceiling. A focal point of the restaurant was the original all-pewter bar that Ward had purchased in auction from the famous Parisian restaurant, Maxim's.

Perhaps, the most unusual attraction of the inn was Herbie's extensive Britannia collection. A devoted Anglophile, he had shelves and display cases that were crammed with china, figurines, and memorabilia from every royal era of England.

*The Black Bass Inn, located in Lumberville, Pennsylvania, just a few miles north of New Hope, was built in the mid-1700s. Needless to say, "The Bass" has its fair share of ghosts.*

Looking at Ward's sovereign acquisitions, one couldn't help but be reminded of the inn's earliest history as a center for Tories who were staunchly loyal to the Crown. But, following the American Revolution, this legendary inn earned a new reputation as a boisterous hang-out for the rowdy men who had been hired to build the Delaware canal. After a hard day's work, the rugged diggers used to stagger into the downstairs bar. Ordering up drafts of ale and flasks of whiskey, the hardy boat men reveled in the raucous atmosphere of this watering hole. According to a legend that has been passed down through the centuries, there was an immigrant worker by the name of Hans who got into a reckless fight with some of the other rivermen and was stabbed to death during the brawl. There have been ghostly reports of a muscular, canal digger sitting at the bar on a stool, and if you look closely, there is a knife in his back. Legend has it that, from time to time, a pool of blood appears on the tavern floor.

Herbie also told me about another strange happening that occurred at the inn one night. A woman who was staying by herself in one of the second floor rooms came flying down the stairs late one night. She was visibly shaken and demanded to see the manager on duty. She could barely get the words out of her mouth to tell him what had happened. Apparently, she was getting ready for bed and had just gone into the bathroom to wash up and brush her teeth. When she came out of the bathroom, she looked up and saw the ghostly figure of a woman dressed in a long, white gown. She was sitting in a rocking chair with a pearl-handed pistol in her lap.

The young woman flew out of the room in a state of shock. She located the night manager and pleaded with him to find her a new room. Since the inn was fully booked that evening, she ended up sleeping on a hard wooden bench down on the first floor. She insisted that the manager stay within close proximity to her all night long. Early the next morning, she asked a member of the hotel staff to accompany her while she returned to the room to pack up her things. She checked out at dawn and my best guess is that she never went back to the "Bass" again.

Perhaps, if you visit any one of these old hostelries, you, too, might experience a chance encounter with one of the invisible residents who still haunt the property. I believe that each one has left in their wake a ghostly trail of past memories.

*

*The Glassmans have been welcoming guests to their award winning collection of historic inns (all situated in the heart of New Hope) for close to thirty years.*

*As mentioned previously, the luxurious, newly renovated Lambertville House is located across the river in Lambertville, New Jersey.*

*Herbert Ward operated the Black Bass Inn successfully for over fifty years. Following his death the inn went through several changes. In 2008, Jack Thompson purchased the inn. After extensive renovations, the Bass has been lovingly restored to its true splendor.*

# THE AUTHOR SPEAKS FOR HERSELF

As I make my slow pilgrimage through the world,
a certain sense of beautiful mystery seems to gather and grow.

*

*Arthur Christopher Benson*

# THE NIGHT THAT CONVINCED ME GHOSTS ARE REAL

Many years ago when I was historical editor for a regional magazine in Bucks County, Pennsylvania, I received a strange phone call.

"Would you be interested in hearing a remarkable ghost story? It's right up your alley. It's about Revolutionary soldiers and you're always writing about them."

I paused, a bit taken aback. "I'm not interested in ghosts. My specialty is history."

"I know," the woman replied, "but this deals with both."

I started to say that since one is factual and the other is fictional, I wouldn't wish to...

Before I could answer, she was into her tale.

"We live off River Road, a few miles above Washington Crossing." She was referring to the historic site on the Delaware River where George Washington and his troops crossed on Christmas night in December of 1776.

"Yes," I murmured, wary of what I might be getting into.

"Well, yesterday evening my daughter and I were in the kitchen when we heard the sound of drums beating. My little girl ran to the front door and called, 'Look, Mommy, soldiers!' I saw her at the screen door, pointing. Curious as to what soldiers would be doing on our back road, I went to see. Sure enough, a company of men in Revolutionary uniforms was marching along to the roll of drums.

"I tried to explain to my daughter that they must be one of those groups of history buffs who re-enact Revolutionary battles. But I asked myself: What were they doing in that out-of-the-way area? Why weren't they performing down at the Crossing?

"Then, right while we were looking at them, marching within a hundred feet of us—they vanished! The whole company of men just disappeared from sight and we were staring at an empty road without a soul on it!"

I wondered if my caller had some mental problems.

Her voice went on, "We live close to that huge old oak tree. You know, the one that bears a plaque stating its age—some five hundred years old, I believe? Now, that's right where Washington's troops encamped before the crossing... right? In the fields by that tree?"

I had to agree.

"Well, I feel my little girl and I saw their ghosts!" I know you may not believe in such things but I want to tell you that we did see them. No one can change that fact."

I thanked my caller for taking the time to phone me but there was nothing really of interest to me in her story. I could not accept it. She was entitled to believe what she wished to believe, but I could never be convinced such an incident could occur. Had she considered that somehow she had been hallucinating? Something had deluded her? Perhaps the twilight shadows or the shape of trees bordering the road...

The woman was silent for a moment.

"I can tell you don't believe me."

"I wish that I could. It's a fascinating tale."

"Alright," she murmured, disappointment in her voice. "Thank you for listening anyway."

That was many years ago. Today I hope that phone caller is reading this story. I would like her to know that for some time now I have believed her story—ever since the night I spent in an inn while vacationing in Scotland. It is a night I have never forgotten. Although it began innocently enough.

I drove into the village of Pitlochry in the Scottish highlands just as dusk was falling. I'd been on the road all day. I wanted to get farther north but with darkness coming on, it seemed wiser not to attempt further mountains. I sputtered to a stop in front of a quaint stone building called logically enough, "Scotland's Hotel."

I trudged inside and leaned against the registration desk. The clerk looked more tired than I.

"I can't help you, madam. Not one mite. I haven't a single room. We're completely booked up!" He stared at me over wire-rimmed glasses. "It's festival time in Pitlochry, you know. We've been thoroughly booked up for over a fortnight."

I took a deep breath. I understood. All the same, I couldn't go on. Wasn't there a small room, a back room, some little corner he could give me?

A pause. A long pause.

"Madam. I have explained..."

"I know. But I just have to stay this one night. Please—look again. See if you can't find me something."

The desk clerk sighed. "Well, there is a little back room."

"I'll take it," I said quickly.

The man reached behind him and grabbed a big metal key. He placed it into my hand, and then pointed over one shoulder. Following the direction with my eyes, I thanked him and made my way down the hall.

When I pushed open the door, a faint mustiness stirred itself towards my nostrils. I coughed and put my suitcase down on an old oak chair. I looked around, if not in unbounded joy, at least in relief. It was obviously an unused room at the rear of some forgotten hallway. But I wasn't going to be fussy. Under the circumstances it looked good.

I walked around the room. There was a rickety night table at the head of the brown-clad bed. A dresser stood like a weary friend in one corner. Facing me were two windows covered wispily with curtains that seemed suspended cobwebs in the gray twilight. Between them stood the only light in the room, an old standing lamp.

I washed in a small bath across the hall, got into my nightgown and fell into the bed with a groan. In seconds I was asleep. For a time. Then I was startled awake. Without knowing what had aroused me I was suddenly totally alert. And terribly, terribly cold.

Shivering, I reached down and pulled the spread over me. The air felt frozen and I found my teeth chattering. I wondered how even in the Scottish Highlands, it could get so cold.

Then I heard the creaking sound of the door opening. I lifted my head in the darkness and held it there for long seconds, waiting. I could hear nothing further. Deciding I must have imagined it, I lay back. Tiny fears nagged at me but I reassured myself: I had bolted the door before retiring. I recalled that clearly. I nestled down under the covers wishing myself into a sense of warmth.

But in the next instant, my eyes shot open again. Footsteps were coming towards me, sharp and distinct. The floor boards squeaked eerily with each footfall.

My heart nearly stopped. I couldn't move. I wanted to cry out, "Who's there?" but I couldn't speak.

The stealthy walker reached the head of my bed and stopped.

I lay stiff with terror. I waited. Nothing happened.

Slowly I reached out to the night table and grabbed my flashlight. Summoning all the courage I could, I clicked it on. There was no one there. I zeroed in on the door. It was closed tight and the bolt I had slid across was still in its locked position!

I fell back on the pillow. This was fantastic! How on earth could I have been so sure that someone had come in? I must have been half asleep and dreaming. I turned over on my side, my flashlight in my grasp. Gradually my whirling thoughts calmed down. I drifted off.

Then it came again! The door whining on its hinges as it opened. Footsteps coming steadily towards me, troubling the floor boards into muffled groans. Again they halted at the night stand. Perspiration exploded from my scalp. My mind reeled. This time, there was no mistaking it, someone had come into the room!

My fingers around the flashlight were too paralyzed to move. Nor could I utter a sound. But my mind told me over and over that I was not alone in that room and I must do something!

In a burst of action, I yanked my flashlight out and flicked it on. There was no one. I scanned the door in its ray. It was still closed and locked.

Beginning to doubt my sanity, I pulled into a sitting position and swept the room with a beam of light. The dresser and the tall lamp and the gauzy windows were silent and alone with me. There was nothing else.

Slowly I dragged out of bed. Some animal must have gotten in, perhaps through a hole in the wall or floor. Some cat or some wild thing from the woods and it was in there hiding.

I got up, chilled to the bone, and put on my raincoat. I found the switch on the standing lamp and turned it on. It showered the room with a parchment glow. I began to circle slowly around and around, poking into corners, stooping to look under the bed. Under the chair. There was absolutely nothing in the room but me and the lifeless furnishings.

What was happening to me? I couldn't understand it. I switched off the tall lamp and fell back into bed, raincoat and all. I was exhausted. I closed my eyes in the darkness feeling as alone and helpless as a child.

In the next second I felt my body pull into tautness. My ears strained. Once more a sound was coming through the night. A new sound. The faint rolling of a drum!

I lay there listening with every nerve in my body on edge. Somewhere a drum was beating. How could that be at this late hour? Was there some distant reveler from the festival still roaming the streets?

I slipped out of bed once more and made my way to the windows. I brushed one fragile curtain aside and peered out. There was neither moon nor street lamp. I could see nothing.

But the drumming persisted.

I released the curtain and trudged back to bed thoughtfully.

I could still hear the faint staccato beat as though from some distant military review. But what regiment would be parading around at this hour?

Then just as quickly as it had come, the drumming ceased.

I lay still for long minutes listening and waiting. But there were no further sounds. The room began to grow warmer. Soon I had to take off my raincoat. In utter weariness I dropped down under the covers and somehow in the new and beautiful silence the room was finally offering to me, I fell asleep. I didn't waken until after nine the next morning.

As soon as I had dressed and packed I went to the front desk. A young man with bright blue eyes and blonde hair was in charge. In reply to my questioning about the disturbances in my room he said, "I can't imagine, ma'am, how there could have been noises of any kind. This is a particularly quiet establishment. We're an early-to-bed outfit, don't you know?"

He was all blandness and no information.

I paid my bill, put my bag in the car and looked around. I wondered if there could be a good Scottish tearoom nearby where I could get a bite to eat. I found it a few blocks away. It was a tiny stone cottage with geraniums bouncing in green window boxes.

After devouring a steaming cup of strong tea and a stack of brown toast heavily larded with marmalade, I put down my napkin and sighed with contentment. At that late breakfast hour, I was the only guest there.

"That was delicious," I told the freckled, broad-smiling owner as she came towards me with a freshly brewed pot.

"Aye," she beamed, "there's nothin' equal to the bracin' one gets from a good cup o' tea. Are ye from the States, lass?"

I told her I was and that I was on holiday and had come to see the storied land of Sir Walter Scott, beautiful Bobbie Burns and Bonnie Prince Charles. Quite naturally then my conversation led into my mentioning the previous night's experience.

The woman's plump-cheeked face grew suddenly serious. One hand on the edge of the table, she leaned curiously over me.

"Ye heard all o' that?"

I nodded and she straightened.

"Well, why wouldn't ye now, lass? After all, ye are nigh to the famous Pass o' Killiecrankie!"

"Pass of what?"

"The Pass o' Killiecrankie just outside o' town. 'Tis the ravine where many a soul on a dark night has heard and seen the phantom soldiers o' Bonnie Dundee chargin' the Redcoats!"

*Battlefield ghosts have allegedly haunted the Killiecrankie Pass in Pitlochry, Scotland, since 1689.*

My mouth dropped open. The sandy-haired woman pulled out the chair opposite and sat down.

"'Tis not fable, lass. 'Tis history. The Battle o' Killiecrankie on July 27, in..." I caught my breath and she stopped speaking. This was July 27! The woman nodded. "Aye," she continued, "'Twas July 27, in 1689, when King William's forces attacked the Highlands. He wanted to rout the Jacobites once an' for all an' be free o' fear that King James would e'er return but ..." She pulled back and smiled, "It didn't work. Na' by a lancer's heave, I can tell ye! John Graham of Claverhouse, Viscount Dundee, was too much a match for the thin-livered British. He an' his roarin' Highlanders charged down these mountain walls, trapped the scarlet coats in the pass an' sent them sprawlin' to their deaths!"

I shook my head, listening to this woman of Pitlochry describe a battle hundreds of years old as though it had just taken place yesterday.

"Now, lass," she looked intently at me, "mayhap, you didna' ha' the chance to see the phantom soldiers, tucked away as ye were, but ye did hear them! Ye see, 'twas just off this high road that the Dundee forces camped the night afore the battle. An' all night long, 'tis said the Highland chief couldna' sleep. He paced back an' forth afore his tent an' didna' give the order to charge 'till dusk."

I leaned forward to catch every word.

"... an' though the Tartans sent the British runnin' in minutes, 'twas long enough for the Bonnie Dundee to catch a shot in the side! He died that night." She tilted her head. "Now, do ye suppose that ye heard the ghost of Dundee as he walked? An' heard the drums o' his charge into the dusk?"

I turned and glanced out the window at the heather-hued hills.

"I don't know. I just don't know what to think." I got to my feet. Thanking my tearoom hostess for all she had shared with me, I paid her, then walked thoughtfully back to my car.

I drove straight to the Pass. I had to see the history-laden spot for myself.

It was a rock-ribbed ravine with early afternoon light sifting through the cathedral-tall trees. I heard nothing in those moments but the calls of hidden birds. I wondered, did the beating of the drums disturb their lofty nocturnal sleep?

I looked around at the smooth-faced boulders and the leafy sides of the precipitous pass. I could in my mind's eye see and feel every defending Highlander fighting for his causes. Were they any different from the American Continental soldiers of a near-century who took their bleeding footprint stand against the Redcoats in my Bucks County corner of the world?

I climbed back up towards the high road. My thoughts raced. Could there be a connection between my sensitivity to our Revolutionary soldiers and those of far away Scotland? Could my love of the lore of one put me in a kind of psychic rapport with the other? Particularly since I had arrived at the site on the anniversary of the eve of the battle?

Was there much more for me to learn of time and space and the power of thoughts (subconscious as well as conscious) and the oneness of such thoughts regardless of distance or century?

As I drove away from Pitlochry I began to recall that strange phone call from the woman who had told me so vividly of her experience with the phantom soldiers. I knew now she had told the truth. Ghosts *are* real. Not spirits from another world but thoughts re-activated again from some great pool of consciousness shared by everyone throughout time.

In that quiet back room of the Scotland Hotel I believe that I tuned into a past trauma. Why that particular room? Who knows… perhaps, some visitor had once received word of the loss of a loved one in war. That experience, superimposed on the centuries-old tragedy of Dundee's death, lit a kind of forever fire of remembrance, locked in immortal dusk, in the atmosphere of that room.

I have never forgotten that hotel. Nor the ghostly Pass of Killiecrankie or the fresh-faced Scottish woman who so wondrously shared with me a part of her country's past.

Today I often visit the ancient white oak of Washington's encampment here in Bucks County. Five hundred years have given it an unparalleled magnificence. And to me, a certain air of mysteriousness exudes from it over the surrounding countryside.

Not for me alone, I hasten to add. Only a short time ago I received a phone call from an old friend of mine, Louise McCarthy. She told me she and her husband had just moved to an old house off Windybush Road. I recalled that is only a short distance from the old encampment grounds. I asked her how she liked living there.

"Oh, we love it," she answered, "except occasionally at night I find I can't get to sleep. I keep hearing the sound of a drum beating."

And I believe her.

*

*Killiecrankie in Perthshire, Scotland, is renowned for both its history and scenery. "The narrow pass between high mountains with the Garry River flowing beneath in a deep, dark foam, and a rocky channel overhung with trees, forms a scene of horrible grandeur," wrote Thomas Pennant in 1769. The magnificent wooded gorge, where "the bones of heroes rest," is allegedly filled with battlefield ghosts. Tourists can visit a number of key battle sites: Soldier's Leap, Troopers Den, and the Claverhouse Stone which marks the place where Viscount Dundee was killed.*

## SOMEONE IN MY STUDIO?

For many years, I rented a room on a long-term basis at the Lambertville House. I used the room exclusively as a writing studio. It was the perfect environment—a quiet space of my own where I could hone my craft without any interruptions. It didn't take much effort to transform this small room into my own personal office space. My needs were simple: a desk for my trusty old typewriter and some empty shelves where I could stack up my collection of books and research documents. To make the room seem homey, I added my favorite old rocking chair and some photos of my family. Room 305 was my own little private writing Mecca. Best of all, I could pop downstairs for quick bite to eat whenever I felt the need for a little pick-me-up.

It was in this room that I churned out the manuscripts for my first ghost books—*Ghosts in the Valley*, *More Ghosts in the Valley*, and *Ghosts of the Revolution*. While I was working on these books (each one featured a collection of true hauntings and supernatural happenings), I was struck by the possibility that I might experience some paranormal activity myself. But, nothing unusual ever happened.

And, then one day things changed. I decided to write my first book of fiction. It would be a ghost story that I could maneuver and plan. I could invent the characters and plot out the tale from start to finish. That would be fun and a change. No prescribed incidents and endings that I always had to stick to in writing up true happenings.

*A number of strange occurrences took place in the author's writing studio.*

I began to mull over some possible interesting plots. In no time at all it came to me. I would write about a young teenage girl who felt she was the reincarnation of an Egyptian princess. The girl would be an unhappy child. Her mother would be either divorced, or dead, and she would be living in an old Bucks County stone house with her father and his new wife, a woman about forty.

One beautiful spring day, I arrived at my studio and wasted no time in sitting down at the typewriter to begin this story. I had a rough, penciled outline of the plot line, chapter by chapter, at my elbow. But as the afternoon wore on, I found myself consulting the outline less and less. When I returned to my studio the next day, I realized that I wouldn't be using it at all. In fact, as soon as I sat down to write I was overcome with a very strange feeling. The words just seemed to spew out of my typewriter. I began to have a somewhat awed awareness that I wasn't doing the writing after all.

From then on, every day, I felt as though I was merely sitting in front of the typewriter, watching and waiting. There was nothing for me to do but hit the keys in my usual two finger "hunt and peck" style.

As time went on, the plot began to take on a very bizarre twist. The teenage daughter was fading from the story. For some reason, she was receding into a background role and the middle-aged woman was becoming the central character.

I thought to myself, "This is definitely not what I had in mind. I've got to rework this story and tone down the woman's part." But I couldn't. The wife only became stronger and more central to the plot.

To be honest with you, she was not a character that I liked. And, the husband was even worse. "Where did these people come from?" I asked myself. And, then there was the woman's father who entered into the plot through flashback scenes. He was the most monstrous character of all. He was a brute who had beaten the woman so badly as a child that she had become disfigured for life. Of course, she was mentally and emotionally scarred as well. She harbored such a hatred of her father that, in mature years, it became an overriding obsession.

After finishing about half of the book, I sat back and shook my head in wonderment. What a peculiar story. It was certainly not the one I had intended to write at all. The reincarnated Egyptian princess had become reduced to little more than a sub-plot. The strong flow of the father-daughter hate theme being projected by the older woman was now the main subject matter. I said to myself, "That's it. I'm stopping right here. I don't want to write about that woman and her terrible relationship with her father."

I stopped at the climax point of the writing and left my studio for about four days. I had to go out of town on business. Not surprisingly, the whole time I was gone my mind kept going back to that strange story. I could not shake away the pain of that tormented woman. For some reason, her agony stayed with me.

When I returned to my studio a week later, I was greeted with stories of weird occurrences that took place during my absence.

First of all, the chamber maid told me that the whole time I was away she heard a typewriter going behind the closed door of my room. The sound of the typewriter continued late into the night (I normally left my studio early in the evening so that I would be at home on time to have dinner with my husband), so the maid decided to check out the room. The minute she opened the door and looked in, the sound stopped abruptly. She found it incredible that the room was empty.

"It was unmistakably the sound of your typing, Mrs. Jeffrey— kind of irregular in rhythm." I smiled and nodded, always the first to admit that I am probably the only professional writer who has never learned to type properly.

"And, that's not all," said Edith. "When I went into the room to replace the towels on your sink rack, I felt like there was a strong force tugging violently at the towels from the opposite direction. I was doing a real tug-of-war with that little critter before I realized what was going on. You better believe that I dropped those towels as fast as I could and got the heck out of there."

Marty had more to add to her tale.

"I was in there the next day cleaning when I suddenly heard a creaking behind me. I turned around and looked in the corner and there was your old Victorian rocker moving back and forth, back and forth—all by itself!" Marty shook her head. "I didn't run out though. I figured it was just some old soul who hadn't left this world completely yet. I didn't think that he or she was going to hurt me. But instead of just sittin' there, the least they could have done is give me a little help. I looked over at that rocking chair and said, 'Why don't you get up outa that chair and help me clean?'"

The night clerk at the front desk had his tales, too.

One night the adjoining room to my studio was rented to a lone traveler. In the middle of the night, she came downstairs and complained that someone in the next room was trying to get into her room through the interconnecting door. She said that the door kept opening and banging against the chair and the standing lamp fixture in her room. Naturally, she was very frightened.

The desk clerk explained to her that the door was always kept locked on both sides. Furthermore, no one was ever in the adjoining room at night—it was rented to a writer who only used the room in the daytime. Nevertheless, the lady kept insisting that someone was in there. The night clerk followed her upstairs and went into my room. It was, of course, empty. But, he did notice that the door between the two rooms was open. He bolted it shut again and then he checked the lock on her side of the door. He assured his hotel guest that all was well. After a sleepless night, the woman packed up her things at the crack of dawn and checked out.

Indeed, they were puzzling stories although I had no doubt that these strange things had occurred.

And then one day I opened my studio door and experienced something odd myself. I found the rocking chair in the middle of the room and the interconnecting door wide open. I moved the chair back to its proper place, closed the door and locked it, and then got on with my work. Each time I entered my studio for the next few days, I discovered this same perplexing pattern of disturbance. I made a point to check with the desk clerk, the floor maids and the housekeeper to see if any of them had moved things around in my room or had reason to open the interconnecting door but, of course, they all said no. Nobody had touched a thing.

In the meantime, I finally succeeded in finishing up the unpredictable story I had been working on. Somehow, my first piece of fiction had evolved into quite a distasteful story. I gladly stuffed the manuscript into a large envelope and set it aside to deliver to my typist. As I was leaving my studio room that afternoon, I happened to run into the head housekeeper who was in charge of all the rooms in the inn. Mary had worked at the Lambertville House for many, many years. We stopped in the hallway to exchange pleasantries and then I decided to ask Mary a question which had been swirling around in my mind for a long time. "Mary, can you remember something? Did anyone unusual ever occupy this room of mine years ago?"

Without a moment's hesitation, Mary answered, "There sure was. I'll never forget 'em! There was once a father and daughter who rented out those two connecting rooms for a couple of months. What an odd pair they were. So nasty and disagreeable. And you know what? That woman hated that father of hers with a passion. That's all she wanted to talk about when he was out of earshot. 'He's nothing but a tyrant,' she'd say, 'cold and abusive.' She absolutely despised him.

"Lots of weird things were going on while they were staying here. We'd hear them yelling and shouting at the top of their lungs. They would get so mad at each other that they'd start throwing things. I had to sweep up broken glass in those two rooms more than one time." Mary shuddered. "I'll tell ya this. We couldn't wait until those two checked out. When they were finally gone, we all thanked the Lord."

I nodded as Mary told me this story. I finally understood what had been coming through my typewriter keys for all those past months. Clearly, there was a story that lingered in the thought environment of that room. A story that I had been subconsciously "picking up" minute by minute. A tale of hatred and loathing that finally got told.

The book, which I entitled *Hand of Hate*, was never published. It still lies in a bottom drawer unread and as unknown as the troubled father and daughter who once occupied adjoining rooms on the third floor of the old, historic Lambertville House.


## MY NIGHT IN A HAUNTED MOTEL

After twenty-five years of studying ghosts and investigating psychic phenomena, I have learned to listen closely. Now, as I was talking to Douglas Johnson, an engineer with a prominent Philadelphia firm, I was listening with all my might. He was telling me the story of a nightmare he'd lived through several years earlier while traveling in Virginia on business.

He'd sent for me to see if I could make some sense out of the strange events he'd experienced. "When I awakened at dawn," Doug was saying, "a tremendous weight was pressing on my chest. I couldn't see it, but it was so powerful I thought I wouldn't be able to breathe another second. I clenched and unclenched my fists and tried to roll over, but I couldn't budge. This terrible force was crushing down on me, harder and harder, until I felt my life being squeezed out of me. Right there, in that strange bed hundreds of miles from home, I was sure I was going to die!"

Doug Johnson swallowed hard. "You *do* believe me?"

"Every word," I assured him.

He twisted uncomfortably in his seat. He was hesitating and I knew why. Tales of ghosts and hauntings are acceptable from writers and artists, but not from engineers.

"I've never told anyone about this before."

"I can appreciate how you feel," I said. "But don't worry. To me, an experience in a haunted room is neither strange nor inexplicable. Please continue."

Doug cleared his throat and went on, "Just as I thought I would surely expire from lack of oxygen, the weight lifted. I couldn't believe what I was seeing. Suspended over me was a black form—a badly misshapen figure with grotesque stumps for arms and legs, and a face like a smashed-in bulldog's with violently distorted features. I lay stiff with shock. Then, slowly, the thing began to rise. Suddenly, without warning, it vanished!

"I lay there for long seconds before I realized the room was ice cold. I was shivering. Then gradually the air got warmer and my heart began to beat steadily again."

Anyone looking at Doug Johnson would size him up as a levelheaded man, practically impossible to intimidate. Yet that night in the Virginia motel, *something* had almost frightened him to death. What had it been?

Doug had come to his own conclusion. "There was an evil spirit in that room with me—there had to be!"

I shook my head. "I don't think so," I said. "There was something there all right, but I suspect it was a thought force of some kind rather than an evil spirit." My years of research into psychic phenomena had convinced me that thoughts can be *things*—we not only think them, we can see, feel, hear and touch them. Thoughts are like echoes. They linger long after the incident to which they are connected.

"When a person experiences a traumatic event, he or she feels a powerful emotional response," I explained. "This response remains behind in a kind of psychic ether. Days, months, even years later, when another sensitive mortal steps into that mental atmosphere, they will pick up or tune in to these thoughts. It's much the way a person tunes into the sound waves all around him on his radio. If you're one of the people able to pick up thoughts out of the atmosphere," I told Doug, "your mind will re-enact the scene that once took place."

"What do you think took place in that motel room?"

"I don't know," I replied. "But something happened there and I'm going to find out. I'm headed south next week to do some research, I'll make a point to stop at that town in Virginia and stay in that same room."

The motel was next to an old bridge that crossed a glistening expanse of the Appomattox River. I checked in at dusk and asked for the same room Doug had occupied. Luckily it was free. It was small, with the usual furnishings: double bed with tweedy bedspread, long, low chest, a small closet with three wire hangers. On one wall hung a dark-framed mirror, and over the bed a picture of a dirt path winding through a wood. There was a tiny bathroom with a stall shower. Within minutes I had my small suitcase unpacked, was undressed and ready to step into the shower. As I pulled back the shower curtain, I thought I heard a sound from the bedroom. I paused and listened. Dead silence. Still, I had a distinct feeling that I was not alone. I slipped on my robe and went back into the bedroom. A figure at my elbow sent my senses reeling, until I realized it was nothing more deadly than my raincoat hanging outside the bathroom door! I smiled to myself for such foolishness. But the feeling of another person persisted.

I went to bed before 10:00 p.m., weary from a long day's driving, but far from exhausted. In fact, I felt quite expectant. Something was waiting there to be realized by me. I lay in bed wondering what it might be. I could almost feel my eyes and ears tingling with anticipation in the darkness.

Then it happened.

An indistinct sound came from the door at the left side of the room. I listened hard, every sense alerted. Gradually the sound grew louder. It was a series of gasps. Someone was making a desperate effort to breathe!

I lay perfectly still and listened. I knew that no one was at my door breathing with difficulty. I knew I was alone—yet not alone. A memory was there trying to talk to me. I didn't move a muscle. The struggling breaths ceased. Then I heard the sound of something heavy—like a body, too weighty to be carried—being dragged across the floor. Finally, the slow dragging came to a stop.

Then I saw the figures. There were two people at the foot of my bed. One was a dark-haired man of about twenty years old, and on his back he carried a small blond boy of about seven or eight. The boy's head was soft and limp. His arms hung over the older man's chest.

My mouth opened, but I couldn't speak. Anyway, I knew there was no need to. Then the two forms faded into the night. I closed my eyes briefly. When I opened them, another scene revealed itself. The metal jaws of a bright yellow crane were trying to pick up a large piece of wreckage. Then the crane vanished.

The next morning I inquired of the desk clerk, the chambermaid, and the motel owner whether any unusual or traumatic events had taken place at that motel or in the neighborhood over the years.

From the desk clerk I got an uncomprehending stare. The chambermaid told me there had been a train derailment in a town about twenty miles away a few years before. "No," I said, "I don't think that what I'm looking for would have occurred that far away."

I persisted. I found the motel owner and spoke to him. I told him I knew there was a train track close by because I'd heard the train whistle at night. Had there been a wreck on that line? He thought a moment and shook his head. Nope. Had there ever been an accident involving tractor trailers or large trucks on the highway in front of the motel? No, the motel owner couldn't recall any.

I left the haunted motel and made my way to a nearby plantation that was on my list of places to visit for research into psychic phenomena. I told the owner about my night in the motel room, ending with my opinion that an accident involving a large vehicle had occurred close by.

Suddenly she sat forward in her chair. "You're right," she said, "there was! Sometime in the 1930s, when I was a little girl, a big bus carrying a load of passengers skidded on that bridge and broke through the guardrail. The bus plunged into the river and everyone on board was killed." She put a hand on my arm. "And I clearly remember, it did take a huge crane to pull the wreckage out of the river!"

Hours later I drove to Richmond and made my way to a local newspaper office where I spent hours looking through old clippings. At last I found what I was looking for. In December 1935, a large interstate bus went into a skid on the old bridge and plunged over the rail. The bus driver was crushed to death behind the wheel. Before a rescue could be attempted everyone had drowned.

*The author believed that a fatal accident could leave behind super-charged, psychic vibrations.*

Now I had an explanation for the puzzling phenomena in the little motel room. Doug Johnson and I had psychically picked up on that earlier tragic event. Our subconscious minds had tuned into those past happenings and relayed the information to our conscious minds. Doug was able to feel the dark, crushing weight against his chest that the bus driver had experienced in his last moments. I'd heard the sounds of people trapped underwater in the bus and trying to get their breaths. And then I'd tuned into the sounds of the bodies being dragged up the embankment. And, finally, I'd seen the crane that was used to lift the crushed bus.

The accident was a matter of journalistic record. It had actually happened. But I could not find any information about the dark-haired rescuer I had envisioned or about the little blonde-haired boy on his back.

Why did these experiences reveal themselves to a few of us who had stopped at that motel? I suspect it's because of empathy, the capacity to feel very strongly what other people feel. Not everyone who comes upon a haunting site experiences the paranormal. Only those of us who have a sensitivity to a past trauma are able to tune it on it. Then there's another reason that could explain why I saw those past events so clearly. I have deeply buried memories of another automobile accident—one in which both of my parents were killed twenty-five years ago.

After completing my newspaper search in Richmond, I called my husband (who works for the same engineering company as Doug) and told him the whole story. "Please ask Doug if he ever drove a bus or a truck," I asked him. "I feel he did and that's why he could pick up what the bus driver went through that day."

"I don't have to ask him," my husband said. "I can tell you right now. He does drive a truck on occasion. In fact, if any of our equipment has to be shipped in an emergency, it's Doug who handles it."

There you have it.

Today, Doug still shakes his head in wonder at the experience. And I keep searching for stories and proof of even more "inexplicable" events. What may seem incomprehensible, or even impossible to most of us is, to people who value it, a special and private communication between a past event and a person in the present who can re-experience it.


## It Takes Guts To Be a Ghost Hunter

As I was flipping through the Philadelphia Evening Bulletin many years ago, a very short article tucked away in the back pages of the newspaper happened to catch my eye. The headline read, "Beria's Home Now Moscow's Most Haunted House." The article went on to describe some of the terrifying ghostly manifestations that had been reported at a home which was once the former residence of Lavrenty Beria, the bloodthirsty Soviet Secret Police Chief who served under Joseph Stalin. A blurb at the end of the article mentioned that in 1958, the State had turned the gruesome, old house into an embassy and passed it off to Tunisia, a small nation located in North Africa.

Needless to say, this story piqued my interest. I cut out the article and carefully filed it away for future reference. Although, I must admit, a thought was already churning around in my mind, "Add it to your To Do list, Adi. There's another ghostly place that you just have to see for yourself."

My psychic investigations had already taken me to some very remote parts of the world, although, let's be honest, going behind the Iron Curtain in 1969 was another thing.

For an American citizen to consider making a trip to Russia during the years of communist rule was almost unheard of. My husband quickly dismissed the idea with three little words, "Are you crazy?" But, there was such a chilling fascination to this spooky house located behind the Kremlin walls that I just couldn't get the idea out of my head.

I spent hours at the library pouring over any material I could find related to Stalin's reign of terror and, in particular, his right hand hatchet man, Lavrenty Beria. Dubbed "The Bloody Butcher," he was, undoubtedly, one of history's most reviled men. From the 1930s through the 1950s, Stalin, along with Beria and the rest of their political cronies, were responsible for slaughtering close to twenty million Russians. Innocent men, women and children were sent to the scaffold, executed by a firing squad, deported to Siberia, or to Beria's own fiendish delight, tortured to death or savagely murdered right in the confines of his Moscow home. This beast of a man also had a special weakness for women. It seemed he saved his most atrocious acts of brutality for young teenage girls. After being lured into his grim mansion, these poor innocent victims would be beaten, raped, and then sent down to the basement to be murdered by one of Beria's henchmen.

Reading these accounts sent shivers up and down my spine. I could just imagine the shroud of evil that still hovered over this deathly place. Now, more than ever, I was determined to see "Moscow's Most Haunted House" for myself.

I announced to my husband that I was going to be making a trip to the Soviet Union either with or without him. He looked absolutely horrified. But, being the caring and protective man that he is, he eventually agreed to go with me.

We waited months to obtain the legal documents and proper visas that we needed. In the meantime, I sent a letter to the Tunisian

*In 1969, Adi-Kent Thomas Jeffrey traveled to communist Russia to investigate "Moscow's Most Haunted House," the former residence of Lavrenty Beria.*

Embassy in Africa asking if they would be kind enough to forward me the exact address of their diplomatic offices in Moscow.

As the time drew near for us to depart, my husband was filled with anxiety and trepidation. I, on the other hand, felt exactly the opposite. Although I was well aware of the potential dangers ("Be very careful, Adi. Don't mention to anyone that you're a writer—and no political discussions whatsoever." "Look over your shoulder at all times—an American visitor to Russia is always under suspicion."), I couldn't help but feel a surge of excitement and exhilaration. After all, I had been anticipating this adventure for a very long time. As a researcher, I knew that there was no substitute for on-the-ground, firsthand investigation.

Armed with my Berlitz book of Russian phrases, a wealth of information about Lavrenty Pavlovich Beria that I had stored in my head (in those days, anyone entering the county had to give sworn testimony to Soviet officials that they were not bringing in printed materials of any kind—no books, newspapers, magazines, or written documents), plus an address furnished to me by the Tunisian Embassy (which I had memorized), my husband and I set off on our trip to the USSR.

It was clear from the moment our plane touched down in Moscow that we had entered a communist country. Right away, a foreign visitor could sense the totalitarian influence that the State operated over everyone and everything. Life was strictly regulated and the rules were enforced. We were made to wait in a long queue for what seemed like an interminable amount of time. Stern looking government officials examined our documents and the contents of our luggage carefully and thoroughly. After getting the last stamp of approval, we were finally released to go on our way. As we checked into our small hotel located a couple of blocks away from Red Square, I was filled with a great sense of satisfaction. At long last, I was here!

During our first few days in Moscow, a Russian Intourist guide escorted us around the bustling city. We were thrilled to see the famous landmarks—the Kremlin, Red Square, Lenin's tomb, the Karl Marx monument, and St.Basil's Cathedral (my favorite) with its bright colored onion-shaped domes and redbrick towers. We were mesmerized by the exquisite dancing of the Bolshoi ballet and we smiled in amazement as we watched the ice skating bears perform their stunts in the famous Moscow Circus.

All of these attractions were sensational sights to see, but my heart was still pounding in anticipation for what I hoped was yet to come.

With all the courage and confidence I could muster up, I finally approached our guide with my long-awaited question. "Anya, could you please give me directions to this address?" She stared down at the piece of paper on which I had printed out the number and street name of the Tunisian Embassy—1/28 Katchalova. "Why do you wish to go there?" she asked immediately. "Oh, I have a date for tea. You see, my brother had the privilege of visiting your country a year ago and while he was here one of Ambassador Najib Bouziri's consulates invited him for afternoon tea at the embassy headquarters. My dear brother has already made the necessary arrangements for me to do the same." I swallowed hard, making sure to give no visible sign of my nervousness.

Anya turned over the piece of paper and drew me a simple map on the back. Whew! I had gotten through the first hurdle.

I had made up my mind that we would brave the walk no matter how long it was. I was fearful about hiring a taxi driver who might be suspicious of this particular destination. Who knows? In Russia, a cab driver could very well be a KGB agent.

As we left our hotel, all I could do was hope and pray that all of my advance planning would pay off. Before leaving on our trip, I had sent a handwritten note to the embassy consulate giving him the same spiel about my older brother coming for tea and asking if my husband and I might be able to enjoy the same privilege when visiting Russia in the spring. I was overjoyed when I received a formal and gracious reply from the Tunisian Embassy stating that we would be most welcome.

My heart was pounding as we turned down the quiet, residential street. Although the old mansion had now been painted with pleasant shades of sky blue and snowy white, I, for one would not be fooled. I knew the horrid truth of what had once taken place behind this pastel façade.

True to their word, my husband and I received a cordial welcome as we entered the foyer and were ushered into the ornate drawing room. The walls were covered with stunning works of art, a richly gold patterned carpet covered the floor and the room was filled with solid mahogany Victorian furniture. A most hospitable gentleman who introduced himself as "Rami" gestured for us to please sit down. My throat was so dry from nervousness that I found it hard to speak. I took a few sips of the strong mint tea to help moisten my mouth. I had no appetite for food at all, but I tried my best to nibble on the sweet pastries and fresh figs which they had spread out before us.

As much as I appreciated the embassy's warm hospitality, I really didn't want to waste too much time eating and drinking. I had more important matters on my mind. I knew that it was now or never.

Leaving my husband at the tea table, I excused myself and asked Rami if he might direct me to the toilette. Once the two of us were out in the main hallway (as fate would have it—we were all alone), I turned to him and in a hushed whisper said just one word... *"Beria!"* There was not a moment's hesitation on his part. He nodded his head to let me know he understood and then signaled for me to follow him.

I will never forget this moment as long as I live.

Rami led me down to the bowels of the basement. My footsteps followed his as we descended into the dark, subterranean cavern of cellar rooms. An iron door with two huge, flat metal bolts marked the entrance into one of Beria's infamous torture chambers. Chills ran through my whole body as Rami pointed out the heavy steel shackles still nailed to the walls. In another recessed area, he showed me the scorched walls which still remained blackened after all these years. (Beria used to take a blowtorch to his victims as a way of getting a confession out of them.) My mouth dropped open when I stepped into a cold, damp room filled with large porcelain tubs. My mind raced back and forth trying to conjure up what atrocious function they could have served. Did countless, unnamed people once drown to death in these tubs? I soon got my answer. Apparently, after Beria gave the orders to his henchmen to shoot a victim in the back of the head, they were then instructed to dispose of the body in an acid filled bath. I was reeling with the horror of it all.

Rami, who had been with the embassy staff for over a decade, went on to tell me that bones had been found in the backyard, the cellar, and hidden behind walls. "We know this building holds hate. Bad things have happened here. Very bad. We hear loud screams. We hear people crying." Apparently, the most common apparition seen in the building is a young, naked girl who runs down the corridor with her mouth open wide, screaming silently. She vanishes just before reaching the front door.

This sojourn into the Lavrenty Beria's bloodcurdling underworld was beyond anything I could have ever fathomed.

I felt absolutely numb by the time I stepped back into the drawing room to join my husband. "Are you okay?" he asked. I shrugged my shoulders in an attempt to disguise the shudders that were going through my whole body. I gave him a quick, non-verbal clue—one of those wide-opened looks of shock and disbelief—and then regained my composure the best that I could. We finished up our tea, thanked our host profusely and then the two of us began the long walk back to our hotel. Neither one of us said a word. Even after we were ensconced in the privacy of our own hotel room, my husband put his index finger to his lips. We knew this was serious business. I had just seen concrete evidence of the murderous crimes committed by a former Head of State. I also knew that the Soviet government took retribution against anyone who dug up information that they wanted to keep secret. Our lips were sealed.

It wasn't until we reached West Berlin that I was finally able to breathe a deep sigh of relief. Freedom at last. And a chance to tell about my spine-chilling tour of Beria's stone-dungeons where, to this day, I have no doubt that tormented spirits still shriek and moan and cry for help.

Who would have thought that the Soviet Union would eventually collapse? It is hard to believe that this all powerful police state has gone through such a dramatic transformation. Glasnost has drawn back the Iron Curtain.

Beria is dead.

Communism is dead.

But, evil does not go in peace. Horror lives on.

I am convinced that there will always be ghosts wandering through "Moscow's Most Haunted House"... for they are the ones who will never let us forget.

*

*For many years, my mother was a member of the National Speakers Bureau. I adapted this story from one of her most popular lectures entitled, "The Dark Side of Russia." It is interesting to note that for decades after Beria was shot (December 23, 1953), every record of his evil doings was expunged from official Soviet histories. It is only after the collapse of communism that the truth started to emerge.*

## THE IRON DOOR

Ghost hunting in Great Britain can be a wildly fun and richly rewarding experience. Steeped in history, England is teeming with legends of restless spirits, strange hauntings and supernatural tales.

Over the years, I have spent a considerable amount of time searching for ghosts who seem to lurk everywhere across the spectral landscapes of this country. And, I have not been disappointed. Ghosts are plentiful. You'll find them hovering in city alleyways and sinister passages, in dark and foreboding ruins of castles, in quaint countryside villages, across misty green fields, all the way to the fog-shrouded coastline.

London, in particular, is a multi-cultural metropolis that seems to be pulsating with ghosts. It has often been called "The Ghost Capital of England."

One of the most interesting London ghost stories that I've researched is the "Widow in Black," a well-known ghostly entity at the Duke of York Theater on St. Martin's Lane.

The history of this haunted theater dates back to 1892. The grand, three-tiered, neoclassical structure was the first theater to be built in the West End section of London. It was built for Frank Wyatt and his wife, Violet Melnotte. Violet, a former actress, was the theater's first proprietor. Following her husband's death, she stayed on to manage the theater. Known to everyone as "Madame," she was reportedly a cranky, old bird who served as the driving force behind the theater until the day she died in 1935.

A strong, dominating woman with an iron will, she had the final word in all matters. Legend has it that when "Madame" heard about a man who had attempted to commit suicide by gassing himself in the gents' toilets (he was spotted in time and taken to the hospital), she immediately dispatched someone to the hospital to find out his name and address. As a matter of patient privacy, the hospital staff refused to divulge any information about the man. When Madame Melnotte got word of this, she fired back, "Well, who is to pay for the use of the gas?"

I was not surprised to learn that this eccentric, dictatorial woman, who literally ran the show at the Duke of York Theater for over forty years, was still finding ways to make her presence known at her old stomping grounds. Why should a little thing like death stop Violet Melnotte from taking charge?

During one of my recent London ghost hunting expeditions, I purposely bought tickets to attend a show at the Duke of York Theater. Not only did I look forward to seeing a great stage production, I was also eager to see if "Madame," or any other resident ghosts, might be enjoying the show along with me. I didn't pick up any ghostly vibrations that night, but I was able to make an appointment to speak with the general manager of the theater.

My meeting with this gentleman proved to be very interesting. Of course, he spoke first about the well known spirit of Madame Melnotte. "She's usually seen in the dress circle bar," he said, "outfitted completely in black from head to toe. I'll be frank with you—in all my years at this theater I've never seen her, but, supposedly, she's here."

When I asked him if he had ever heard about any other strange occurrences in the theater, he paused for a moment, nodded his head, and then proceeded to tell me his own story.

"Yes, a real weird experience took place here that frightened me out of my wits the first time it happened," he said. "It was during

*Violet Melnotte (1855-1935) was the owner and proprietor of the Duke of York Theater in London, England.*

my early tenure as manager. The year was 1974, I'll never forget it. Alan Bates was starring in a show called *Life Class.* The second act was in progress. I was sitting upstairs in my office and all of a sudden I heard a loud, crashing noise. It sounded like a metal door being slammed shut. I got up and rushed into the corridor. I couldn't imagine what in the world was going on. I quickly scurried downstairs. I checked out the auditorium and the foyer. Everything was calm and undisturbed. I checked with the stage door keeper. She hadn't heard a thing. There was one clerk still on duty in the box office, so I questioned him. It was clear he had no idea of what I was talking about. He looked at me like I'd gone barmy. So I turned around, went back upstairs to my office and dismissed the noise as simply an 'odd occurrence.' Well, unfortunately, that was not the end of things. The next night, at exactly ten minutes after ten, the same thing happened. I heard a very loud clamor that sounded like the reverberations of a heavy, metal door being slammed shut. Once again, I inspected the theater premises and came up with nothing.

"The following day, I gathered a team together to go through the entire theater with a fine-toothed comb. And, what do you think? We came up with nothing. We knew that in the original construction of the building, the dressing rooms were located in a detached building connected to the theater by a short, covered iron bridge, but that was long gone. We carefully searched through all four stories of the building and I can assure you—we did not find a metal door anywhere in this entire building!"

But, according to the general manager, he heard this non-existent, metal door slamming shut every theater night at precisely ten minutes after ten. "The timing was precise," he told me. "It was predictable and brilliantly scary, as well." This went on for over a year. One night, he finally decided that he couldn't take it anymore.

"I'm telling you—it was driving me bloody mad! I made my way down to the first floor box office and as I stepped through the little brass entrance way there, I just blurted out to the clerk... 'I can't take this one more night! I simply *can not* take this!'"

With those words, he saw something bright flashing in front of him which was followed by the sound of an object hitting the floor. He leaned down and picked up a heavy, old-fashioned key with a tag on it. He had never seen the key before in his life. He examined it closely. The identification tag said "IRON DOOR."

He showed me the key which at the time he had hidden away in one of his office drawers. "The moment that key came into my possession," he said, "the nightly disruptions stopped."

As I thought about this intriguing story, it was easy to make some kind of psychic connection between the unexplained noise (a metal door slamming shut on its own) and Madame Melnotte, the original proprietor known for running the theater with an "iron hand." The fact that at one time a metal bridge existed in the theater (which presumably had a door attached to it at one end or the other) was another piece of information that seemed to fit nicely into the psychic puzzle. But, what about the timing? Why did this disturbance occur at precisely ten minutes after ten every night? That was the question that the theater manager and I pondered out loud together.

I told him it was my feeling that something tragic occurred in the theater at that time. Perhaps, it was even the culminating tragic part of a play. The tragic event, or crisis, may have occurred hundreds of years ago, but since we know that tragedies leave the strongest memory impressions, it was my belief that the theater atmosphere was still charged with an enormous psychic energy.

*A mysterious incident at the Duke of York Theater involved a key marked "Iron Door."*

At the mention of the word "tragic," the manager was prompted to tell me about another interesting occurrence of paranormal phenomena associated with the theater's history. He turned to me and said rather matter-of-factly, "Did you know that we are home to a costume that tried to kill?"

I swallowed hard and said, "No, I didn't. Please tell me more!"

"Way back in the 1920s, our wardrobe department rented a ladies jacket. It was a tight-fitting, black, bolero jacket. The actress, Thora Hind, wore it for her leading role in the new play *The Queen Came By*. Apparently, this was no ordinary jacket. Thora complained that the jacket grew tighter and tighter on her as the play went on. After one scene, she came running backstage yelling 'Get this thing off of me! This jacket's trying to squeeze me to death! I can't breathe!' Every single actress who wore the jacket suffered the same feelings of constriction and suffocation. Another actress complained that she felt the collar around her neck trying to strangle her." The bolero soon became dubbed "The Strangler Jacket." Needless to say, the mere mention of a black bolero sent every actress reeling.

In an attempt to find out if this "killer" jacket had any connection to the spirit world, a séance was held in the theater. The medium contacted the spirit of the young actress who first wore the garment. She related a story about a jealous boyfriend who had strangled her to death inside a theater while she was wearing the jacket.

According to the theater manager, no one has been able to confirm that the incident the medium described ever took place. But, it seemed plausible to conclude that the infamous "Strangler Jacket" (due to whatever cause) did contain a residue of malicious thoughts and energy.

With many thanks and a final "cheerio" to the theater manager, I left the Duke of York Theater with an avalanche of new information to think about and mull over. And, after my European sojourn was over, that is exactly what I did. I decided to start by doing a little research on the play *Life Class* written by the British playwright, David Storey. As you may recall, this was the stage production going on when the "slamming door" incident first began. Interestingly enough, the play involved a nude model who posed for students in an art class. During the second act of the play, there was a powerful rape scene.

Was this violent bit of stage action the dramatic "crisis" that triggered the theater manager's subconscious thought? Did this particular scene take place a little after ten-o-clock each night? Perhaps, without knowing it, he was tuning into Madame Melnotte's dormant energies. Was she letting him know that she was still in charge and that she disapproved of such a controversial scene being re-enacted in her theater night after night? One can easily imagine the strong-willed "Madame" slamming a metal door as means of amplifying her extreme displeasure. Did this man, unconsciously, pick up Violet's anger and project it as the sound of a screeching interruption? Did the large, old-fashioned key materialize at the very moment when the theater manager felt enough internal rage to declare—"This has got to stop," thereby announcing he was in charge, and not the "Madame"?

Or then again, might the sound of the banging door connect in some way to the distressed actresses struggling to get free from the "Strangler Jacket?" Did they rush across the bridge leading to the dressing rooms in a panic slamming the gate behind them? Were they making a hasty stage door exit sometime around ten p.m.?

These are all questions and thoughts that have churned through my mind at one time or another. Isn't it marvelous that we can never exhaust the mysteries of the supernatural?

The grand finale to my interview with the Duke of York's manager was the surprise souvenir he handed me as I was leaving the theater. Slipping the infamous key to the "Iron Door" in my hand, he said... "Jolly well. The 'Madame' of the house can haunt *you* from now on if she likes."

Thank heavens he didn't decide to send me home with the "Strangler Jacket."

\*

*The Duke of York Theater, located at 104 St. Martin's Lane, has seen many notable events. In 1900, Puccini saw David Belasco's one-act play here entitled "Madame Butterfly" and was inspired to turn the tale into an opera. The inaugural flight of Peter Pan occurred on the stage in 1904. Charlie Chaplin made his theatrical debut when he was 14 years old in the play "Sherlock Holmes." In 1908, Isadora Duncan performed what was considered a "scandalous, bare-legged dance" on the public stage of the theater. Today, Violet Melnotte is credited for converting the West End district of London into a new theatrical center. She continues to play her favorite role as resident ghost in her former theater. Presently owned by the Ambassador Group, the graceful, four-level Duke of York Theater is considered a Victorian jewel.*

*It is interesting to note that in many modern theaters a "ghost light" is left burning on the stage all through the night. (In Shakespeare's time, it would have been a candle.) Now it is a single, bare light bulb and its purpose is to keep the ghosts at bay.*

*This story concludes with an amazing coincidence. At the time this book went to press, the current production at the Duke of York Theater was "Ghost Stories."*

# IT RUNS IN THE FAMILY

The only real valuable thing is intuition.

*

*Albert Einstein*

# HELEN WAS DEAD RIGHT

*Miss Helen Rowe*

In the year 1901, a young lady by the name of Helen Rowe was living at 937 K Street in Washington, D.C. One day Helen and her close friend, Sara Sterling, decided to pay a call on a well-known, fashionable dressmaker who lived nearby. Her name was Ada Gilbert Dennis and her dress designs were quite the rage in Washington, D.C. Her dressmaking establishment was patronized by women of the highest social circle in the city, wives and daughters of government officials and foreign diplomats. Every stylish young girl and every woman of high personage thrilled at the thought of a Dennis gown.

Mrs. Dennis and her sudden rise to success in the fashion world had become the talk of the town. She was known to be a woman in her late forties and a widow. Her husband, Walter Dennis, an actor, had died several years before. After his death, she opened up a fashion establishment on the first floor of her home which was located at 1117 K Street. She was doing quite well with a staff of twenty seamstresses. She was so absorbed in her business that she had little spare time for anything else.

In anticipation of the upcoming holiday season, which was always a time of merriment and festivity in the capital city, the two young ladies, Helen and Sara, decided that nothing would make them happier than to appear at one of the Christmas balls wearing an original Ada Dennis creation.

On Monday evening, December 9, around 7:30 p.m., the two young girls knocked on the door of the dressmaker's brownstone house. A servant let them in and ushered them through the vestibule into the front hallway. A sign hanging on the thick paneled doors to the right said, *"Good Day. Do Come In. Please Wait In The Parlor."* They were told that Mrs. Dennis was finishing up her dinner but that it wouldn't be a long wait. As Helen and Sara stepped into the front parlor, the room was dimly lit but the atmosphere seemed gracious and inviting. A divan, several tufted easy chairs, and a collection of small side tables were arranged in front of the fireplace. A large mirror surmounted the mantel. There was a Victorian loveseat covered in wine velvet which obviously had seen many years of service. A round, walnut table in the middle of the room was covered with sheet music and other papers. In one corner of the room, an old rocking chair had been placed in front of a huge sweeping fern which rose up from a brass jardinière on the floor. There were bookcases lining the walls. Every inch of the floor space seemed to be covered. A large étagère, and a music cabinet, as well, had been squeezed into the room. Looming from the window corner of the parlor, the girls' eyes were drawn to a baby grand piano with a round, spin-top stool tucked beneath its keyboard. A gas chandelier provided illumination, but it was quite feeble for this time of the evening.

The general impression of this room was that it was warm and pleasant although, in truth, it was so cluttered up with furnishings that one could well imagine it appeared dim and shady even during the daytime.

At the rear of the room, heavy velvet drapes separated a back parlor from their view. Apparently, Mrs. Dennis used this area for her own living quarters as her seamstresses occupied the second floor with their sewing machines. The rooms on the third floor had been rented out to four different boarders. The girls had heard about nearly every detail of this fascinating establishment through neighborhood talk.

With nervous anticipation, the girls seated themselves in the front parlor. Sara on the worn-out loveseat, and Helen on the rocking chair in front of the graceful plant. They could hear Mrs. Dennis bustling about in the back parlor. They waited patiently, saying nothing, but casting glances back and forth at each other. They knew that the clock was ticking away and that they were uncommonly late to be calling at this time of night.

All of a sudden, the silence in the parlor was broken by Helen's abrupt movement. She leaped out of the rocking chair as if startled, and clasped her hands around her throat.

"What's the matter, Helen?" asked Sara.

Helen just shrugged her shoulders, and without saying a word, she sauntered over to the other corner of the room and took a seat on the mahogany piano stool. As the moments ticked by and the wait grew longer, Helen swiveled around on the stool and idly let her fingers play across the keys. She was already quite an accomplished young concert pianist so it seemed only natural that she would strike out a tune on the keyboard while waiting. But, within seconds, her hands froze and the music stopped abruptly. Helen jumped up from the piano stool and leaped to her feet.

"Helen, what on earth is troubling you?" persisted Sara.

"This place gives me the creeps. We've got to get out of here right now!" Helen said in a loud stage whisper. Just then, the girls heard the drapery rings slide across the brass rod and Mrs. Dennis stepped into the parlor.

She was a pleasant looking woman, of medium stature, with a round face and gray hair piled high on her head. Her voice was soft and her eyes looked at you kindly. Her gracious smile gave her an air of aristocracy that belied her hard-working occupation. She was known to have a loveable nature. Clients said that she was always very respectful and accommodating, and word was that Ada Dennis was especially good to her employees.

"May I be of assistance?" she asked.

"Oh, yes," Sara replied. "We were hoping that you might fashion each of us a floor-length gown, perhaps with a train?

After much talk back and forth, the girls were delighted with the fair price that she offered them.

"Because you are neighbors," she had said.

Thumbing through the pages in her appointment book, she asked the girls if they could come for fittings at the end of the week.

"How about this coming Friday at three?"

Sara nodded in agreement, but there was no response from Helen.

Why did her friend seem so distracted and preoccupied? Sara just couldn't understand her silence.

Sara took the lead, "Yes, Mrs. Dennis. That will be fine. We will see you then."

Mrs. Dennis walked the two young ladies to the entryway, bid them a gracious farewell and closed the door.

"Isn't she lovely!" exclaimed Sara as the girls walked back down K Street towards their homes. "I can't believe it! At last I'm going have an Ada Gilbert Dennis ball gown to wear! I can't wait to make my grand entrance at the Christmas Jubilee."

But Helen was not listening to a word she said.

"Sara," she interrupted, "I have never felt such horror in any place in my entire life. I couldn't wait to get out of there!"

"What are you talking about?" said Sara. "Nothing seemed strange to me. Sure, the parlor was a little cluttered and the furnishings a little worn out, but who cares? We got to meet Mrs. Dennis and, just think, in a couple of weeks the two of us will be strutting around in our gorgeous new gowns. I didn't have any objection to the place at all. In fact, I thought it was quite appealing."

"It was ghastly," Helen spat out. "I felt as though somebody was trying to kill me! I know that sounds crazy but I swear to you when I was sitting in that corner rocking chair I felt as if there were two hands coming out from that fern and trying to grasp me around my neck!"

Sara came to a standstill. "What a bizarre thing to say! You must be out of your mind, Helen. There wasn't anyone in that room but us."

"I know that," said Helen impatiently, "but all the same, I felt those cold, ghastly hands, and when I sat on the piano stool, my head started to pound and then I felt the most awful pain sear through my whole body. I tell you, Sara, there's something weird about that house."

Helen was dead right.

Early the next morning, at 5:00 a.m., Ada Gilbert Dennis was found in her bed brutally beaten to a pulp. Her skull was crushed, her jawbone broken and her left ear almost severed from her head. Her body was covered with bruises and lacerations. Her clothing and her bed were soaked through with blood. She had been bludgeoned to near death—with a piano stool.

The unfortunate woman, lying in a coma, was taken to Garfield Hospital where she died shortly thereafter.

When Police Headquarters received information about the tragedy, Major Sylvester, the District Chief of Police, along with his accompanying officers and several detectives, went to the house immediately to investigate.

The police came to several conclusions right from the start.

First of all they determined that the killer was already in the house when Mrs. Dennis went to bed for the night.

It was apparent that the assailant must have slipped into the front room sometime before Mrs. Dennis locked the two parlor doors from the inside and headed back to her room to retire. All windows on the lower level of the house locked from the inside. Each window catch was carefully inspected by the police and it was found impossible to open them from the outside. One of the front windows was found open after the discovery of the crime, but that was the one through which the criminal had escaped, not entered. The only entry point into Mrs. Dennis's rear living quarters was through the front parlor.

How did the intruder get into the house?

Since the Dennis house was also a place of business with people coming and going all the time, the police surmised that it would not be difficult for a stranger to slip through the front door by following closely in the wake of a client going into the house. And once in, he (or she) could easily find a safe hiding place in the dimly lit parlor that was crammed with furnishings. Perhaps, the assailant hid under the couch or in a corner behind one of the big ferns?

The second obvious fact was the weapon used by the criminal. In the middle of the front parlor floor, near the center table, the police found the round top, or seat, of the piano stool. The base of the stool, from which the top had been unscrewed, was lying overturned in front of the piano. This stool was of the type prevalent at the time. The base had three legs and the top had a long, central shaft which screwed onto the base, so that the seat could be raised or lowered.

The condition of the stool top made it only too apparent that it was the instrument with which the crime was committed. There were blood stains not only on the flat surface of the seat, but on the edge as well. This fitted in perfectly with the statement in the medical report, which said that the skull was crushed in on the right side as by a single blow inflicted with some heavy, flat instrument.

What could have provoked the intruder to such a murderous attack?

Months went by, Major Sylvester and Detective Hartigan examined everything and everybody in hopes of finding a clue that would help them unravel this case and answer that question. They poured over every book and paper in Mrs. Dennis' room and workshop. They interviewed her roomers, her seamstresses, her servants, her patrons, and her neighbors. The District Commissioners even authorized a reward for $1,000 for the arrest and conviction of the criminal. But nothing was ever discovered that could connect any person with the crime or suggest any motive.

There were a thousand questions in this horrific tragedy that never would be answered.

It was a ghastly crime.

And, it was Miss Helen Rowe, my mother, who was the first to know that an evil presence was lurking somewhere in Mrs. Dennis' cluttered and dusty Victorian parlor.

\*

*This story was often told to me by my mother. My grandfather, Adolph Alexander Thomas, researched the facts to the Dennis murder case and wrote an investigative account of the crime for Master Detective Magazine in October, 1944. My grandmother included an addendum to his story relating her own chilling experience of psychic precognition.*

# AFTERWORD

The more enlightened our houses,
the more their walls ooze ghosts.

*

*Italo Calvino*

# THE GHOST OF ADI-KENT THOMAS JEFFREY

*Adi-Kent's portrait still hangs in the living room of her former Georgetown residence in Washington, D.C. Not surprisingly, the 1892 townhouse (now her daughter's home) is filled with psychic energy.*

During the last years of her life, Adi-Kent lived in a charming, historic home located in the heart of Georgetown, Washington, D.C. Years after she had passed on, I came to know her lovely daughter, Lynda, who now lives in her parent's townhouse along with her wonderful husband, Curt. To know Lynda is to know her amazing mother. We have spent many hours curled up on the couch in her mother's former living room sharing stories of Adi's fascinating life. Always, there above us, hung a stunning portrait of Adi-Kent. At the time the portrait was painted, she was a young woman dressed in an elegant, royal blue gown. The Georgetown home is still filled with Adi's spirit, as well as her photos, manuscripts, and her priceless collections of all sorts of beautiful things.

Many times, I found myself wishing I could have met Lynda's mother. Then, one night I did. I was spending the weekend with Lynda and Curt. I had gone to bed early as I had a long workday ahead, seeing patients in my D.C. office. I have always slept soundly in their cozy guest room, but one night I woke up in the wee hours of the morning to the rustle of taffeta and the feeling of a presence coming towards me. I sat up to see Adi-Kent walking down the hallway towards me from what had been her bedroom. She was dressed in her royal blue taffeta gown. She didn't break stride as she looked directly at me and said in a commanding tone, "I am Adi-Kent." With that, she turned, proceeded quickly down the steps, and then vanished away.

I had never seen a ghost and until that moment I didn't know whether they truly existed. But that night I knew I had just experienced my deepest desire, to finally meet the incredible, the one and only, Adi-Kent Thomas Jeffrey.

*Dr. Annette Annechild*
*Delray Beach, Florida*

# CONCLUSION

An enchanted life has many moments when the heart is overwhelmed by some haunting quality in the world or by a spirit or voice speaking from deep within a thing, a place, or a person.

*

*Henry Louis Mencken*

# TAKE JOY

"So, tell me the truth, have *you* ever seen a ghost?"

That is probably the question I've heard the most throughout my life. I wish I could answer in the affirmative but as of this date, I have yet to be thrilled, surprised or frightened (I don't know which adverb to pick) by an apparition from the Other World.

Do I believe in ghosts? Of course, I do. How could I not?

I grew up with a mother who was always running off to a tarot card reading, a table-tilting session, or a midnight séance. She spent four decades of her life pursuing the mysteries of this world. When most women in the 1950s were busy being homemakers, my mom was off doing her own thing—she was actively and passionately engaged in being a supernatural sleuth.

When I was growing up, I accompanied my mother on many interviews and research trips. As the years went on, I attended her writing classes, lectures, and publicity tours. No matter what the venue, I can tell you this, Adi-Kent Thomas Jeffrey was always confident, knowledgeable, engaging, glamorous, and totally charming.

I remember the nights we gathered around our small black and white television (adjusting the "rabbit ears" until we got a clear picture) and watched my mother make her grand appearances on both *What's My Line* and *To Tell the Truth*. Who would have ever guessed that this statuesque blonde, dressed in a Molly Parnis black sheath, and batting her false eyelashes at the camera would fess up to being a bona fide ghost buster? My mother was always a delightful enigma.

Growing up as an only child, I was very attached to my mother. She was always my role model for how to live a full, meaningful, balanced, and I must add, an exciting life.

Over the years, the two of us took many mother-daughter trips together. We went here, there, and everywhere—traveling in the States, and Canada, the Caribbean Islands, and Europe. Always with excess luggage and, more often than not, with no definitive plans in mind. My mother used to say, "Let's just pack up and go, darling." Spontaneity was her favorite mode of operation.

One such last-minute excursion that I'll never forget is the summer jaunt we took to Atlantic City when I was a young teenage girl. My mother booked us an oceanfront room at the Chalfont-Hadden Hall, a lovely resort hotel located right along the boardwalk. (By the way, here's a little known fact about my mother. She was born in Atlantic City and as a tiny baby she made her first trip home from the hospital in one of those large, wicker, canopied rolling chairs. I imagine that a friendly attendant pushed my grandmother and her precious cargo slowly and safely down the boards until they reached their final destination—the Chalfont-Hadden Hotel.) Needless to say, from the time she was born, my mother had a lifelong affinity for this seaside resort.

When the two of us arrived in Atlantic City on that hot, July day, we checked in at the hotel, unpacked our bags, and took some time to admire the view from our room before we headed out to walk the boards. My mother insisted that a trip to the shore must always begin with a box of Fralinger's salt water taffy so, naturally, that was our first stop. Of course, we spent some time at the beach soaking up the sun and dipping our toes in the water (neither one of us was too keen on swimming), but the highlight of this weekend trip was a visit to Steel Pier.

Steel Pier was known to be the most magical place on the great wooden way. A visit to this amusement pier was called "A Vacation in Itself." Stretching 1,780 feet into the ocean, it was filled with a multitude of ballrooms, theaters, and arcades. There was non-stop entertainment going on all day long. One could experience the thrill of a Rocket Ride, gaze in wonderment at boxing cats and performing chimps, cheer loudly for the Female Human Cannon Ball, and best of all, watch breathlessly as the High Diving Horse took a forty-foot plunge into the Atlantic Ocean. Steel Pier also showcased the biggest names in talent. The mix was eclectic—including vaudeville, opera, minstrels, big bands, comedians, and all the famous crooners of the day.

Little did I know that my mother had actually done some planning in advance for this particular trip. She had purchased two tickets for us to see Frankie Avalon perform on Saturday night at Steel Pier. I was over the moon! I had many teen idols in those days, but Frankie Avalon was my absolute favorite.

The Marine Ballroom was packed that evening with hundreds of young teenage girls. Frankie took the mike and sang all of his famous hits to the noisy backdrop of his screaming and adoring fans. We had fabulous seats, but of course, who could stay seated?

As soon as I heard the words, "Venus, if you will, please send a little girl for me to thrill... " I popped out of my seat and squeezed my way into the throng of kids crowded around the stage. To this day, I can still remember standing there with my hands clasped in front of my chin, looking up with dreamy eyes as Frankie continued to sing, "Hey, Venus, Oh, Venus, make my wish come true."

To top off the evening, my mother proceeded to navigate her way back stage, as I followed in tow, to Frankie Avalon's dressing room. She talked her way past every usher and pier attendant saying over and over again, "I'm a writer on assignment from Teen Magazine." We finally got into his dressing room and by that time the piece of chewing gum I had in my mouth had completely dissolved. I was so nervous and excited! I couldn't believe my mother had actually made this happen. She had made *my* greatest wish come true! I got to meet Frankie Avalon—it was a thrill beyond my imagination. He shook my hand. He autographed my program. He gave me a moment to remember forever.

When we returned back to our hotel room late that night, I walked out onto our oceanfront balcony, looked out at the sparkling marquee lights posted high on the pier that announced to the world—FRANKIE AVALON IN PERSON TODAY—and I said to my mother, "I will never forget this night for as long as I live."

It was one of those incredibly happy moments that I have stored away safely in the nooks and crannies of my memory bank for a long, long time.

Many decades later, my dear mother reached the end of her journey here on earth. She had no fear of death. "I'm just changing my address with God, that's all." She wanted no memorial service and no fanfare. And, most of all, she wanted no sadness or mourning. She used to quote Lord Mountbatten who once said, "I can't think of a more wonderful thanksgiving for the life I have had than that everyone should be jolly at my funeral."

It had already been decided that my mother's final resting place would be in one of Bucks County's lovely memorial parks. There was only a handful of us gathered together to say our final good-byes, just as my mother would have wanted. My father, husband, cousin, and I drove up from Washington, D.C. We stayed at the Lambertville Station Hotel the night before the service. The next morning, I got up and dressed myself appropriately ("Remember, no black, darling!"), skipped my eye make-up routine, and tucked a linen handkerchief into my purse. With a heavy heart, I stood in the hallway waiting for the elevator to carry our little group downstairs to the lobby. The doors opened, and the four of us got in. The second I stepped into the elevator, what do you suppose I heard? It was the voice of my long-ago teen idol singing the song I still knew by heart... "Oh, Venus, take the brightest stars up in the skies and place them in her eyes for me. Oh, Venus, make my wish come true."

In those brief moments, as the elevator whisked us from our room upstairs down to the main floor lobby, I knew I had just received a message from my mother. "Don't be sad, dear. Remember the good times. Be happy. I want to look down and see stars in your eyes—not tears."

*Life goes on... Lynda Jeffrey shares a joyful moment with her granddaughter.*

Later on, as I pondered this experience, I found it interesting that the Frankie Avalon song was not only a link to a happy time the two of us once shared, but it also evoked a strong memory of

Atlantic City for me. At the time of my mother's death, I feel that she was intentionally sending me a reminder of her birth. It was as if she wanted to reiterate one of her strongest beliefs, "When we die, we are born into a new world, and a new life. To end is to begin," she used to say.

I will never forget those few, fleeting moments in the hotel elevator. It was such a poignant experience for me. And so typical of my mother. I must say, her timing was impeccable. Just before we were to drive out to her grave site, she found a way to remind me that, in spite of our losses, life is still filled with sweetness and innocence, happy times and good memories, and, most of all, joy.

No, I haven't seen a ghost—as of yet.

But I do believe that during those few minutes when I was standing in that hotel elevator, my mother chose to communicate with me from the Great Beyond.

Her message was simple, and it was a reflection of how she lived her whole life;

"No matter what, dear… Take Joy."

# APPENDIX

## Interview with
## Adi-Kent Thomas Jeffrey

*Adi-Kent Thomas Jeffrey; Author, Lecturer, Psychic Investigator*

*Tell us how you got started on your ghost chasing career...*

Many years ago, I was writing a syndicated column for the local newspapers called "It Happened in Bucks." I would write about historical figures, events and places in the area. If the house had a ghost legend associated with it, I would include that in the story as well. I figured that a ghost here and there might add a little more pizzazz to my stories but I really didn't take any of this stuff seriously.

To my surprise, I started getting inundated with letters and calls from people who were eager to tell me about their own ghostly experiences. After hearing one story after another, I have to say—I still wasn't convinced. I just came to the conclusion that there were a lot of flaky people living here in the Bucks County area!

Over time, however, I ended up reassessing my own thinking.

I realized that the people contacting me were intelligent, reputable and highly respected individuals. I reached the turning point when a prominent Philadelphia psychoanalyst got in touch with me and told me his paranormal experience about a chiming clock. It was clear that this man was not hallucinating. He was not suffering from a wildly, vivid imagination. He was not lying to me. He was not an idiot. What he was doing was telling me about an incident that seemed to have no rational explanation.

I decided it was time for me to start stretching the boundaries of my own mind. I was determined to find out more. From that point on, I devoted all of my time and energies to exploring the supernatural. I dropped my focus on history and fixated my attention solely on the paranormal. I studied parapsychology with J.B. Rhine at Duke University (Rhine was known as the "Father of E.S.P."), I worked with the renowned medium, Arthur Ford, and I diligently re-read and reanalyzed the works of Freud and Jung. I was curious to learn more about the workings of the human mind. Year after year, I investigated every haunted site that I could track down, nearby or far away. And, most importantly, I listened openly and attentively as people would come to me saying "Wait 'till you hear what happened to me...."

As soon as I opened my mind to new possibilities, all sorts of strange and marvelous things started happening to me. Whether we recognize it or not, life is multi-dimensional. The truth is that we all have powerful psychic abilities, but most of us suppress them in favor of our normal senses.

To me, there is nothing more intriguing than the supernatural.

*Are ghosts real?*

I believe that ghosts are real, but not in the sense that they are departed spirits coming back to earth to haunt the living. I believe that ghosts are projections from the subconscious mind. They are objectified thoughts. I am a firm believer in the power of thought. To me, thoughts are the most powerful force in the universe.

In the old days, before we knew much about human psyche and the power of the subconscious mind, people didn't know how to explain these strange happenings. They thought it must be mischievous spirits from another world. But, as centuries passed, beliefs evolved. Today we have a much greater knowledge about the workings of the human mind. It was Freud who first gave us the shocking news that we have a huge area in our mind's thinking that we're not even aware of. Nine tenths of our thoughts are subconscious. Think about that. Right this very minute, ninety percent of what's going on in your mind is unknown to you!

As we go about our daily earth-bound lives, we often forget, or we ignore, the power of our subconscious mind. It is a mega-memory bank that stores all of our past experiences. It's a subtle, but powerful, instrument that is orchestrating every detail of our life. And, I firmly believe that our subconscious mind also has the ability to create and project the manifestations we call "ghosts."

I also believe that there is a common substratum of mind underlying our own individual minds. The "collective unconscious" (as Carl Jung called it) is a reservoir of thoughts that exists in some kind of continuum beyond the confines of time and space. It's my belief that psychic individuals have the ability to tap into this universal pool of thoughts.

Yes, ghosts can be very dramatic and colorful and they lend themselves to theatrical effects, but I do not believe in spirits. To me, it is much more exciting, powerful and dramatic to think that man's mind is creating things. The concept of a cosmic unconsciousness which is common to us all is absolutely fascinating to me.

*Should we be afraid of ghosts?*

It's natural to be frightened of things we don't understand, but the answer to that question is "No."

Certainly, the encounter may be disturbing, but ghosts are not harmful.

A ghost can't hurt you any more than a monster appearing in your dreams can hurt you.

I always say, "Don't be afraid of ghosts—it's the living you have to worry about!"

*Why are some houses considered "haunted"?*

I don't believe that a house is haunted by spirits of people who once lived there. I've always liked Brad Steiger's definition of a haunted house. He describes a haunted house as a "storehouse of memories or a repository of thoughts in energy form." We know that traumatic or tragic events leave the strongest imprint in the thought environment. When someone with an active psychic sense enters the house, he or she may "tune in" subconsciously and pick up the energy or the impressions left behind. Perhaps, deep down, that person has an emotional connection or an affinity for what has happened there. After tuning in, the subconscious mind collects this impression and then projects it to the conscious mind as an image, a sound, a scent, or a touch. The sixth sense uses the five physical senses as avenues of expression.

The psychic energy in the house acts as a "trigger" to some deep-seated thought or emotion that's been stored in the person's subconscious mind. Next thing you know, the witness *unconsciously* generates an apparition (an external projection) as a response to the impressions they've received.

*Tell us about a haunted house you've investigated...*

As you know, I receive frequent calls from people living in haunted houses. And, as you can imagine, these people are feeling extremely frightened and perplexed. They're looking for help. I do not perform any kind of exorcism since I don't believe that the disturbance is being caused by either good or evil spirits. But, I do offer my services (for free, I might add) as a "psychic analyst."

About a year ago, I got a call from an Episcopalian minister and his wife who complained that they had a ghost in the house who was causing all kinds of trouble. When I met with the couple, they sat down with me and described all the weird things that had been going on in the house for over a year and a half.

In the middle of the night, they would awaken to the sound of footsteps treading lightly down the stairs. Glasses would tip over and spill without provocation. Toys and dolls would fly off the shelves and land in the middle of the room. During the daytime, when the wife was alone in the house, she would sometimes hear the distinct sound of a child crying "Muuuuther" upstairs in the bedroom. Whenever she rushed upstairs to see if someone was there, she found all the rooms empty. On another occasion, a tiny red plastic house from a monopoly game inexplicably turned up on the kitchen table. The game had not been used in ages. It was stacked on a shelf somewhere in the attic of the house.

The strangest occurrence of all happened one night when they were eating dinner. While they were seated at the dining room table, two small, worn, brass buttons which were marked with a military insignia shot across the room and landed in the far corner.

As I listened carefully to these stories I felt there was something in this woman's own subconscious that was causing these disturbances. I didn't think they were coming from the children in the family. I felt strongly that they were coming from her.

I asked her if she knew anything about the history of the house or about the people who lived in the rectory years ago. "Oh, yes," she said immediately. "I'm familiar with some of the people who've lived here because I've walked around the graveyard and looked at their names on the tomb stones." Just then, her voice trailed off from the flow of conversation and she stared at me and said, "Do you know that there is a child's grave outside of that cemetery? It's not in with everyone else. Who would do that to a child? Who would bury a child in such a lonely place?"

Right away, that remark told me an awful lot.

So I asked her... "Have you ever been a lost child?"

The woman quickly exchanged glances with her husband, and I knew that I had hit a sensitive nerve.

The minister nodded his head and said, "My wife has very much of a 'lost child' in her." Apparently, the woman had spent years in an orphanage before she was adopted. She didn't know much about her birth parents except that her real father was an officer in the Polish Army.

All at once, everything started to come together.

Seeing the lonely grave of a little boy who had once lived in the rectory must have triggered deep and long-ago buried feelings of rejection and abandonment. The monopoly "house" piece appeared because of her lack of home as a child. The military buttons materialized as a symbol of the deep, inward longing she still felt for her real father. The plaintive cry that she heard was her own cry within for her mother... "Where is my mother? Why didn't she want me?" I explained to this couple that all of the paranormal manifestations they had experienced were the antics of a lonely child looking for attention or companionship.

Of course, they were stunned. They couldn't believe that unhappy childhood memories from the distant past could have anything to do with the strange happenings going on in their house at the present time.

"Why, it has *everything* to do with what's going on," I said.

Months later, I did get a call from the minister's wife who told me that all the disturbances in the rectory had ceased. She went on to say that she felt truly peaceful for the first time in her life. So, you see—that's my reward. That's my pay.

*You have stated that you don't believe spirits of the dead can return to earth. I'm curious to know... Do you believe in life after death?*

Death is the inevitable adventure for all of us. And, yes, I do believe in immortality. But, I believe we live on another plane of consciousness where we are not able to communicate with the living.

Let's face it... if spirits could come back, they would all be in ethereal form—not in period costumes. What a person's subconscious grasps is an image of the "ghost" as he or she once appeared in their past life.

My guess is that no one has ever seen the ghost of Oliver Cromwell dressed in his nightshirt. The apparitions projected by the subconscious mind always fit the embedded mental images that we have of someone or something. Ghosts look exactly the way we expect them to look.

*Talk to us about mediums and séances...*

Throughout my career, I have worked with some very talented mediums. There are certainly a number of charlatans out there who call themselves mediums and have no qualms about taking advantage of people, but there are also some very honest and honorable psychics who are committed to doing good works. Over the years, I've known some very gifted and highly attuned clairvoyants. Of course, a medium believes that they are communicating with spirits from the other world, but I have a different take on that. A good medium is, obviously, someone who has highly developed psychic abilities. Their subconscious mind easily picks up information from the subconscious thoughts of others and I believe that's what's really going on. I've attended many séances. I've been to numerous palm readers, tarot card readers, crystal readers, tea leaf readers, you name it—and I think it's all the same thing. It's a psychically astute individual who, I believe, is simply reading your subconscious mind and giving back to you your own deepest fears or hopes. Why do you think so many psychics give dire predictions? What they're doing is tapping into the reservoir of fears that we have stored away in our subconscious mind.

*What do you say to skeptics who proclaim that there is no scientific proof that ghosts exist?*

It's a little difficult to prove scientifically that ghosts do or do not exist. It's like trying to prove love in a laboratory. Each person has to decide for themselves. Skeptics and disbelievers, however, should keep in mind this comment from William Thackeray who once said... "It is all very well for you who have never seen a ghost to talk as you do, but had you seen what I have witnessed, you would hold a different opinion."

*One final question: In all your years of conducting psychic investigations, tell me the truth... have you ever been scared?*
No, not really. People are scared by their misperceptions about ghosts. Once you understand the mechanics of the human mind it takes all the terror of the Unknown out of the situation. As I said, I don't believe in ghosts that enter through our front door... only apparitions that enter through our minds.

*Before we go, tell me, Adi... do you have a motto?*
Yes I do. "Our thoughts shape our lives."

*The above questions and answers were excerpted from Alan Scott's interview with Adi-Kent Thomas Jeffrey, WSNI Radio Broadcasting Company, Philadelphia, Pennsylvania.*

# ABOUT THE AUTHORS

*Adi-Kent Thomas Jeffrey*, also known as "The Mistress of the Macabre," spent a lifetime investigating psychic phenomena and the supernatural. Although she traveled the world to investigate. tales of the uncanny, she always returned to her beloved Bucks County, Pennsylvania, to reflect on and write about her experiences.

During her lifetime, Mrs. Jeffrey published over ten books on paranormal subjects. Her blockbuster hit, *The Bermuda Triangle*, earned the author a number one spot on the New York Times best seller list.

Jeffrey's combined talents as a dedicated researcher, tireless investigator, and masterful storyteller, made her one of the Delaware Valley's most celebrated authors for many decades. In addition to being a frequent guest on radio and television, Mrs. Jeffrey was also a renowned lecturer who spoke with authority on the many facets of the supernatural. She ardently believed that truth is stranger and much more astonishing than fiction.

\*

*Lynda Elizabeth Jeffrey*, grew up in Bucks County, Pennsylvania, and followed in her mother's footsteps ever since she was a youngster. As an only child, she took delight in having many "invisible playmates," which, of course, her mother never questioned. After graduating from college, Lynda found her niche teaching kindergarten and worked as an award-winning public school teacher for thirty years. Upon retiring, Lynda has continued to pursue her own love of writing, devoting time and attention, in particular, to completing the manuscripts her mother left behind. Lynda and her husband, Dr. Curtis Plott, currently reside in Washington, D.C., sharing their historic Georgetown home with two black cats.

# GHOST TOURS OF NEW HOPE

*Adele Gamble, Ghost Tours of New Hope*

In 1982, Adi-Kent Thomas Jeffrey founded the company "Ghost Tours of New Hope." The on-going popularity of the ghost books she had authored impelled Jeffrey to start this new business venture. It was clear that many of her readers wanted to learn more about ghostly encounters. New Hope, with its heritage of history and hauntings, served as the perfect venue for a "walk with spirits."

Mrs. Jeffrey designed an array of fascinating tours including "Ghosts 'n Gifts," "Dinner with a Ghost," "Supper and a Séance," "The Thriller Graveyard Tour" and "Haunted Village Weekend." She took great delight in introducing eager ghost hunters as well as just plain curious participants to the mysteries and the history of New Hope, Pennsylvania.

After Jeffrey moved to Washington, D.C. in 1986, Adele Gamble took over as owner and manager of the ghost tour business. With her reverence for the world of the supernatural and her own finely tuned psychic sensibilities, Gamble has been operating the Ghost Tours of New Hope for more than twenty five years. She has received notable recognition and acclaim for her hard work, enthusiasm and successful accomplishments in marketing and expanding the business. Thanks to Adele Gamble, New Hope has become a prime destination, not only for ghost hunters, but for anyone who is eager to learn the shadowy secrets of this historic village.

For more information, please visit the website: www.ghosttoursofnewhope.com

*

To commemorate the 25<sup>th</sup> anniversary of Ghost Tours, Scott Randolph produced a timeless documentary of the unearthly spirits that haunt the enchanted village of New Hope. The film, hosted by Adele Gamble, features a cast of talented local actors re-enacting some of the most fascinating stories told nightly on the tours.

Experience what it's like to spend a night in the Logan Inn's most haunted room; catch a glimpse of America's famous primitive artist, Joseph Pickett, before he vanishes into thin air; enter the "Bucket of Blood" and marvel at a kindly ghost who seeks to comfort rather than disturb.

This documentary film also includes an exclusive interview with Lynda Elizabeth Jeffrey.

Ghost Tours of New Hope DVD is available at amazon.com and arrivalvideo.com.

# ACKNOWLEDGMENTS

My mother's desire to complete her trilogy of ghost books was never fulfilled during her lifetime. After her death, my father presented me with the unfinished manuscript for *Haunted Village and Valley* and instructed me to "take care of your mother's final work." Although it took quite a while for me to summon up the courage to tackle this project, gratefully I did not have to do it alone. I am indebted to a number of significant people who graciously assisted me along the way.

Endless thanks goes to Virginia Thomas Widenmyer, my mother's sister-in-law and my dear "auntie." Her talents as a professional writer, along with her intimate knowledge of my mother and her paranormal pursuits, provided me with much guidance and information. Without her this book would not exist.

The crafting of this book was made possible by the invaluable contributions of many. First I wish to thank Christy Rosché, a skilled journalist, a brilliant guide and a kindred spirit. Christy's knowledge and expertise helped to get this book ready to send out into the world. I am indebted to her for the endless hours she spent on this project and her enthusiastic support. Thanks also to Ashley McNair, a creative collaborator, who devoted careful attention to the preparation of the manuscript.

I believe the addition of photographs to my mother's final volume of ghost stories has made this book more than she ever dreamed it would be. I am especially thankful for the mystical chain of chance that led me to Jim Milligan, a top-notch photographer, who, believe it or not, worked with my mother way back in the 1960s when she was on the staff of Bucks County Life Magazine.

Jen Rogers, who I had the good fortune to meet while staying at Porches on the Towpath (my favorite B&B in New Hope) contributed her extraordinary talents as a graphic designer. Jen's patience, good humor, and willingness to take on "one more thing" will never be forgotten.

Linda Richters' artful photography, which graces the cover of the book, was another happy serendipitous discovery. I am also grateful for the lovely images Emilee Cluff contributed to this book.

My mother called New Hope "the most haunted village in America. After working on this book project, I would have to say it is also the most *helpful* village in the world! This book was enriched by exchanges with many people in New Hope, both friends and strangers, who aided me with their support and counsel.

Reverend Peter Pearson, of St. Philip's Chapel, responded to each request in a kind, timely manner. Corporal Frank DeLuca of the New Hope Police Department, who decades ago was one of the first to be called to the site of Jessica Savitch's accident, provided me with additional information pertaining to this tragic occurrence. I also wish to thank the host of individuals, John Byers, Chrissie Clawson, Trey Crease, Geri Delevich, Paul Licitra and Scott Randolph who embraced my husband and me with warmth and generosity each time we journeyed back to my old hometown. Special and profound thanks goes to Adele Gamble, my mother's friend and protégé, who has carried on the legacy of her work.

I am very grateful to these special friends who each contributed in a unique way towards bringing this book to fruition: Annette Annechild, who believed in this project from the start and surrounded me with her positive energy and whole-hearted support as well as expert editorial advice; Rhoda Joseph, who reviewed the book in its final stages and helped to refine the manuscript. I give her my deepest thanks for the instructive and insightful comments she offered me along with her never-failing sunny disposition. Thanks also goes to Nolan Haan for his constant solace and support during the long process of working on this book.

I owe a debt of thanks to Ann Madden and Peter Boonshaft for kindly allowing me to use their mother's artwork.

To these women—Jacqueline Banyasz, Toni Gordon, Mary Hoban, Kathy Lawrence, Pat Lonardo, Julia McCaul, Terry Mooney, Michele Plott, Peggy Snyder, Helen Stolgitis, Linda Sutliff, Boots Thompson and Susan Vreeland—who went beyond the call of sisterhood to help me whenever possible, my gratitude for your unwavering support cannot be put into words.

My greatest debt of gratitude goes to my husband whose love and encouragement gave me the inspiration to dig out this buried manuscript and get to work. I have no doubt that Adi *dash* Kent sits on her golden cloud and blesses you from above.

Finally, I would like to express my heartfelt thanks and love to my father. His determination to see that my mother's last book would not remain unfinished and unnoticed emboldened me to take on the challenge of this posthumous publication.

Especially and always... I am grateful to my mother.

The intimate, loving relationship I shared with her was my greatest inspiration. I felt her comforting presence and guidance with me every step of the way as I worked on this manuscript. This book is a tribute to her memory and to her beautiful spirit.

If I should die and leave you awhile,
Be not like others, sore undone, who keep
Long vigils by the silent dust, and weep:
For my sake turn again to life, and smile,
Nerving thy heart and trembling hand to do
Something to engage hearts other than thine;
Complete these dear unfinished tasks of mine,
And I, perchance, may therein comfort you.

*

*A. Price Hughes*

# CREDITS

Bailey, George: Photographer
*Coryell House (page 34)*

Boonshaft, Rochelle: Illustrator
*The Searching Ghost of Bonaparte (page 24)*

Bower, Brad: Photographer
*Witch ball (page 55)*

Cluff, Emilee: Photographer
*The Fortune Teller of Ferry Street: jewelry (page 84)*
*The Iron Door: skeleton key (page 149)*

Deans, Alexander: Photographer
*Someone In My Studio: AKTJ (page 130)*

Dreamstime images:
*Haunted stairway (page 19), Knight's helmet (page 21), Siberian Husky (page 60), Eiffel Tower (page 77)*

Halsey, Raymond: Illustrator
*Marie Bordner (page 80)*

Harrison, Elizabeth: Photographer
*Adi-Kent Thomas Jeffrey & Adele Gamble (page 97), Appendix: AKTJ at microphone (page 173)*

IStock images:
*George Washington engraving (page 11), Empress Josephine (page 29), Aaron Burr (page 33), Bells (page 109), Killiecrankie Pass (page 126), Typewriter (page 132), Bus wreck (page 138), Soviet Union Flag (page 141)*

Krist, Bob: Photographer
*Adele Gamble of Ghost Tours (page 182)*

London National Portrait Gallery:
*Violet Melnotte (page 147)*

Milligan, James: Photographer
*Tunnel underneath Bucket of Blood (page 38), Regent's Row house (page 41), Historic Toll House building (page 49), Logan Inn (page 53), Bucks County Playhouse (page 57), Canal & towpath (page 62), Marbles on countertop (page 72), Hexie Hammerstein (page 86), McKonkey Ferry Inn (page 95), Thompson-Neely House (page 100), Bowman's Hill & Tower (page 102), Centre Bridge Inn (page 105), Wedgwood Inn gazebo (page 111), Lambertville House (page 114), The Black Bass Inn (page 116)*

The following photographs are reproduced with the generous permission of their owners:

# TRILOGY OF ADI-KENT THOMAS JEFFREY'S GHOST BOOKS

*Book One: Ghosts in the Valley*
An unforgettable collection of true ghost stories. This enduringly popular book includes encounters with spirits, poltergeists and phantom creatures of many kinds who once haunted and, in many cases, still haunt the homes and highways of one of America's best known areas—the Delaware Valley.

*Book Two: More Ghosts in the Valley*
More fascinating tales of mysterious happenings in the Delaware Valley area. Read about authentic spooks, haunted houses, and psychic disturbances. More than 30 supernatural escapades are whimsically documented in this second volume of ghost stories.

*Book Three: Haunted Village and Valley*
Published posthumously by the author's daughter, this book offers readers one last chance to join Adi-Kent Thomas Jeffrey for a spooky walk along the dark side of the Delaware. With a special emphasis on the lingering ghosts of New Hope, (including photographs), along with a section devoted to the author's own psychic experiences, this book includes 33 astonishing and authentic stories of supernatural phenomena.

# ALSO –

*Across Our Land from Ghost to Ghost: Authentic Ghost Tales From Sea to Shining Sea*
Mrs. Jeffrey shares with you more than two dozen authenticated ghost stories collected on her nation-wide search for spooks, specters, and other eerie manifestations. Read about... ghosts that haunt our nation's capitol, shadowy tales from the South, wild hauntings from the West, nerve shattering stories from the New England area, and dark encounters along the East coast.

All titles also available at amazon.com, bn.com, and at selected regional book stores.

Visit the author's websites

*

www.ghostsinthevalley.com

www.hauntedvillageandvalley.com